JUDITH OLNEY'S
ENTERTAINMENTS

A COOKBOOK TO DELIGHT THE MIND AND SENSES

JUDITH OLNEY'S
ENTERTAINMENTS

A COOKBOOK TO DELIGHT THE MIND AND SENSES

FOREWORD BY
GEORGE LANG

PHOTOGRAPHS BY
MATTHEW KLEIN

DESIGN BY
MILTON GLASER

Woodbury, New York • London • Toronto

ACKNOWLEDGMENTS

With appreciation to: Carol Boyles, Brenda Brodie, Alice Dorman, Jo Oldham, Judy Thompson, Olivia Wu, The Design Gallery, Fowlers of Durham, A Southern Season, and Tranquil Corners Antiques for their help. Thank you also to Ruth Pecan at Barron's, for her continuing support and encouragement.

To Karen Radkai and Penelope Wisner.

All inquiries should be addressed to:
Barron's Educational Series, Inc.
113 Crossways Park Drive
Woodbury, New York 11797

Library of Congress Catalog Card No. 81-14892
International Standard Book No. 0-8120-5410-5

Library of Congress Cataloging in Publication Data

Olney, Judith.
 Judith Olney's entertainments.

 1. Entertaining. I. Title. II. Title: Entertainments.
TX731.O44   642'.4   81-14892
ISBN 0-8120-5410-5   AACR2

PRINTED IN THE UNITED STATES OF AMERICA
12345   048   98765432

CREDITS:
PHOTOGRAPHY: Matthew Klein, unless otherwise noted
JACKET AND COVER DESIGN: Milton Glaser, Inc.
BOOK DESIGN: Milton Glaser, Inc.
EDITORIAL: Carole Berglie
MANUFACTURER: Parthenon Press

TABLE OF CONTENTS

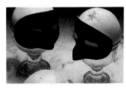

FOREWORD

by GEORGE LANG

I guess the first party was rather small. Eve was the hostess and there was just one guest. For awhile, not much happened worth reporting, though I imagine the eventual invention of the claypot, which made cooking for large numbers of people possible, marked the beginning of the real party era.

Eve set such an effective example that several ladies followed in her footsteps. Hatshepsut, the queen of Egypt some 3,500 years ago, was perhaps the greatest disciple of them all. Like most rulers of note, she had many titles, but "Renewer of Heart" characterizes her best. The organization and subtlety of her parties were legendary.

One of the better moves the Romans made was bringing women to the banquet table. The Roman empress Calpurnia had as many as a dozen honored guests instead of just one, and she served to each his or her favorite dishes.

Not much happened between the Roman glory and the Renaissance. At one of Catherine de Medici's parties in 1549, everything ordinary or vulgar was eliminated, and the foods were only delicate birds like egrets, swans, and herons or specially grown miniature vegetables.

Facts and apocrypha have a way of getting confused when it comes to the times of the great Louis's of France, but apparently Madame du Barry, the courtesan who became Louis XV's mistress, once gave a glittering party full of typical period overkill. After dozens of main courses were served, the tables were removed and, underneath, fabulous flower gardens appeared. Guests were served dainty sweets in a garden setting without moving an inch from their luxurious chairs.

All the great party-givers I have mentioned until now were women. Interestingly, the next three are also of the same gender, but my reportage can take on a personal nature since I knew these women to various degrees.

Perle Mesta always came up with ideas for parties that made everybody happy—and that still is the key to successful affairs.

Elsa Maxwell was the greatest impresario of them all. She forever did the unexpected: from a Barnyard Party at the Waldorf, where she rode into the ballroom on a pink baby elephant, to a quiet little dinner when Cole Porter played his latest songs. The age of spectacles ended with dear Elsa, but since good parties, like ideas, are immortal, she'll always be remembered.

Then there came a time when everyone began to talk alike, to wear identical blue pants, to give parties with foods as little different as possible from those at the party they attended the day before. But just when the cookie-mold approach was most prevalent, a young woman came along and, with sure-handed imagery, she made entertaining Entertainment again. Actually she realized that no one person could do it alone, so she shrewdly enlisted the services of others. Thus the book that became the catalyst in that woeful age was a collaboration among Ms. Olney the cook, Judith Olney the teacher, and Judith the party conceptualizer and bridgebuilder between art and good food.

She wrote a book, the one which you are holding in your hand, about the joy of giving pleasure. Most books on celebrations are echos of past echos from long ago. *Judith Olney's Entertainments* shows what can happen when innocence and sophistication, a superb knowledge of cooking, and the ability to tickle our pleasure bone (why only funny bone?) are combined. Her recipes celebrate simplicity; they are perfect examples of how to straddle the uneven bar of practicality and imagination.

In this volume you will find the whimsical chartings for twenty possible pleasures and gentle lessons on how to use *all* your senses. You will find great art, art that makes you feel a little closer to the angels. And when art is combined with food, you begin to feel the breath of the winged creatures. The book could have been written by Colette, by Cocteau, or by Yuen Mei, the nineteenth-century Chinese poet-cook, but fortunately for us it was created by the contemporary food fantasist, Judith Olney.

INTRODUCTION

This book admittedly is a personal vision of food and its presentation. It draws its inspiration from literature and paintings that have moved me; from meals I have attended; from sources as diverse as a Naples street scene or a chocolate domino glimpsed in a candy store window. In so doing it touches on anthropology and psychology, on music and art, on ritual and drama. And because it is so personal, it could only be honestly photographed in the real setting of my home and workaday kitchen, not in an anonymous studio.

This book is about Entertainments, and I choose that word rather than *entertaining* (which to a cook means planning a suitable meal and serving it to guests), because the word *entertainments* suggests and embraces additional elements of theater, of artistic endeavor and stagecraft, of fantasy and diversion.

That food and its consumption bears parallel relationships with drama and spectacle is not a new concept, and books about historic gastronomy are full of tales of Roman parties and medieval feasts that offered guests not only a steady procession of bizarre and imaginative foods, but also acrobatic feats and musical interludes, wild animals, and poetry between the courses. Of more interest to me is the drama of food and eating in our own lives, for there is no portion of our daily existence that is so mannerized, so ritualized. (Indeed one of the first social lessons in the mannerly life of a child is how to behave, how to play a role, at table.)

When food and eating become social or communal experiences, the drama becomes even more apparent, for all the subtle, sensitive interrelations among people eating and enjoying (or not enjoying) abound. One has only to recall the dramatic tensions at a forced accumulation of in-laws during a holiday meal, at a celebratory wedding feast, or at a wake; or the nervousness one feels before certain cocktail parties. (Will anyone notice my entrance? Will I say my lines correctly?) Is not that dread, perhaps, a form of stage fright?

If guests are the actors in the drama of a social occasion, then the host (or hostess) functions as the producer/director; and it is the host, as Brilliat-Savarin declares, who is responsible for the happiness of the guests as long as they are beneath his roof. If guests bring with them the tensions, the heavy baggage of the day, then the host must recognize and lighten their emotional burden with soothing ambiance, soft music. The host/director must have a subtle understanding of the needs and desires of the guests and of their relationships to food. He must, as it were, understand the psychology of the characters who comprise the cast. Like a good director, he is a master at the art of recognizing the moment, the right time for everything (yet he knows the folly of planning too much.) He understands the art of making the most of the unexpected, of subtlety, of generating energy, and he knows the necessity of using every element of stagecraft at his disposal to sustain his visionary art.

The creative host uses light to advantage, and, in the following Entertainments, you will be advised to use amber-yellow bulbs to cast antique patinas over scenes; to use rose-colored lights when aiming to seduce; to throw the background into obscure shadow to highlight a single, still life centerpiece. (And shadow is just as important as light when creating atmosphere.)

The director/host scores the Entertainments when necessary with music, which can start a party to good advantage by brightening dreary spirits, and then sustain the mood by providing a subdued *obbligato* to unify the evening. He considers pattern, color, and tactile values in plates, linens, and centerpieces, and learns from artists and designers to recreate a variety of scenic effects that range from the realism of a Flemish still life to the impressionistic haze of a Monet water lily garden.

The desired result is an Entertainment—a dining party at the very top of its imaginative possibilities. Like a theatrical staging, a party unfolds for the first and last time according to coincidence and often despite choice or planning. Each one is different, each calls for dissimilar responses from the actors/guests, each necessitates certain readjustments in its audience. The pleasures afforded are of varying degrees, never of one kind. And each occasion's success depends upon a multitude of variables, from the cooperation and participation of the guests (the casting of the party is therefore of vital importance), to the choice, presentation, and progression of the meal.

If we think of the progression of dishes in a meal in theatrical terms, then the Japanese Nō drama springs immediately to mind. An evening of No theater consists of several short plays produced in one program, the order of which is of greater importance than the content of any individual play. Thus a decorative pattern is formed, a sequence of feelings, as each play is presented with a view to its place within the total harmony of the evening. Like a series of plays within a play, are then dishes produced and presented during a meal. Each has its order within the sequence and, in a well-executed meal, those individual dishes will build and grow into a pattern that in the end signifies contentment and harmonious completion.

The successful Entertainment will leave one finally with impressions of wit and freshness, with a multitude of quick kaleidoscopic sensations: arrival, joy, color stimulation; comfort, reflection, repose; sweetness, coolness, warmth; distant music; breaks, twists, shifts; wickedness, laughter, and farewell.

It only takes the dart of the imagination at play, and one need never suffer or impose a dull dinner party again in life.

How to Use This Book

The Entertainments that follow provide a variety of occasions appropriate to different seasons, times, and guests. There are summer meals, winter meals, meals for children, for children and parents, for the entire span of generations. There are Entertainments plotted to evoke moods, responses, emotions—from snug familial camaraderie, to deliberate seduction, to escapist fantasy. There are feasts for multitudes and intimate occasions for lovers. There are breakfasts, lunches, cocktail parties, and dinners, all of which I have used in my own entertaining career or presented in cooking classes.

These Entertainments are dependent on imagination rather than on great monetary expense. All they basically demand for their execution is a sense of humor, a certain style, and, because style needs leisure to be appreciated, time. Each contains within it a small element of drama from the lighting of a cigar, to the climatic scattering of flower petals over an entire table, to the crowning of a king for the evening. You can inform guests of the thematic thread of the event before hand, or simply offer them the Entertainment, saying nothing. (Perhaps the latter way is better, for it allows for and ensures those elements of surprise and amusement that are such pleasant additions to living.)

To stage these events, I frequently use my kitchen, a large open space that was formed, when the house was purchased, by combining the garage with the existing kitchen. It serves well for large groups and informal occasions. (One piece of furniture in the kitchen is a large armoire holding jams, homemade bags of herbs, bottles of potpourri, and candy for children. To give a guest a small remembrance of an occasion is to seal the event large within his memory.) The miniature dining room accommodates a variety of intimate parties (see Appendix); and the remainder of the house, from living room to front hall to bedroom, has also been used at some time for entertaining. Scout your house carefully for interesting locations.

Plan your Entertainments as carefully and easefully as possible. Have the recipes with all their steps firmly in mind, and do not hesitate to modify or simplify if need be. Note that the majority of desserts are chilled or frozen or are fresh fruit; that first courses can usually be made ahead. Take care of all decorative arrangements at least a day before. And finally, if you are without help, be prepared to be on duty throughout the Entertainment. It is a good trick to be a guest at your own party, but it is an act which I do believe is impossible to perform.

Staging with an Artist's Eye

Jan Dazidsz. de Heem, *Still Life*. Metropolitan Museum of Art, Charles B. Curtis Fund, 1912

THE FLEMISH STILL LIFE DINNER

The Inspiration

. . . the laden tables of food and flowers painted so lovingly by the Flemish masters.

A study of any book of still life paintings can give one a multitude of usable ideas for individual place settings (a poached egg in an eggcup on a round wooden board, with fingers of dark bread, a goblet of wine, a small bowl of salt, and a single candle); for buffet arrangements (a table half covered with a red patterned cloth, half with a white damask cloth on which you can still see the folds, tall burnished vases at the back, an elegant compote holding slabs of butter, platters of fruit interspersed with many small dishes repetitively containing cherries, a few berry branches placed here and there); and for centerpieces (wine glasses—stem ends in the interior—blossoming from a delicate basket, an apple and a cabbage suspended from the ceiling on strings above a ripe, cut-open cantaloupe).

THE FLEMISH STILL LIFE DINNER

Early still life paintings, which often contained skulls and books and guttering candles, were intended to teach a moral lesson: Vanity, Vanity, says the preacher, *sic transit gloria mundi*. Even early pictures of meals on tables suggested the passing glories of the world with their blemished fruit and insects poised and ready to devour the spoiled flesh. In the 1600s came a rise of purely secular still lifes, and I particularly enjoy those painted for the Dutch bourgeosie, with their unabashedly opulent displays of earthly goods and rich, succulent foods. The better the painting, the more the sensuous intensity of the objects is captured. The artists strove to fully define flowers, down to the dew drops glistening on their petals only for that moment in time. Butterflies cannot resist the pungent nectar of their roses. Small mice creep into the pictures to nibble on dropped almonds. And if one can look at the paintings and scent the flowers or the salt sea smell from a dish of shellfish, then the viewer himself becomes a part of the scene.

In the most alluring paintings, the artist further invites the senses and the eye of the viewer by animating his composition with a lemon spiral or a napkin or a knife hanging over the edge of the table, which one need then only grasp to begin the meal.

Setting the Scene

As the visual effects of this menu take some time and bother to prepare, it is easiest to hold the guest list to four or six in number. Darken the dining area and, if possible, affix an amber theatrical gel over whatever light does exist, or eat the entire meal by candlelight. Dine on a dark, plain wood table, or select a cloth that is rich and dark. (Satinlike lining fabric in brown or burgundy is cheap and easily obtained.)

In the center of the table place a large basket of flowers and greenery to serve as a holder for the crisp cookie bugs and butterflies, which are propped among the leaves and around the basket base awaiting dessert time. Alert guests that they must come to dinner promptly when called, then set about arranging the first-course lobster plates so that people will be greeted with the handsome sight when they arrive at table. After guests are seated, let them right their wine goblets when the host pours the wine. When the first course is cleared, remove the white napkin under the plate.

Serve the steamed vegetable plates with a gravy boat of Sauce Choron on the side. The fruit plates also make a pretty still life when placed on table. (Always displace some element of the composition and move it toward the viewer/eater.)

Choose heavy cut-crystal glasses or golden stemware for the wine. (I use a collection of six unmatched gold and silver goblets collected inexpensively over a period of time from antique stores.)

Have a background of Baroque music playing: Boccherini, Vivaldi, Albinoni, Torelli, Bach.

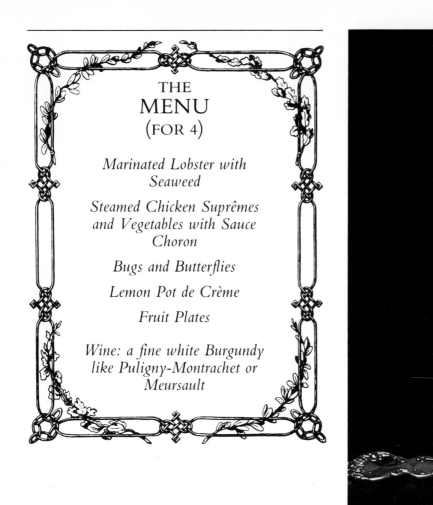

THE
MENU
(FOR 4)

Marinated Lobster with Seaweed

Steamed Chicken Suprêmes and Vegetables with Sauce Choron

Bugs and Butterflies

Lemon Pot de Crème

Fruit Plates

Wine: a fine white Burgundy like Puligny-Montrachet or Meursault

Marinated Lobster with Seaweed

Dried seaweed (Japanese Naruto Wakame, available in oriental or
    gourmet stores)
4 live lobsters, each 1 to 1½ pounds

Court-bouillon:	2 cups dry white wine
	2 tablespoons salt (preferably sea salt)
	1 tablespoon peppercorns
	1 stalk fennel, *or* 1 teaspoon fennel seeds
	3 to 4 stalks parsley
	1 bay leaf
	1 small onion, sliced
	1 small carrot, sliced
Marinade:	3 large shallots, sliced thin
	1 small can tomatoes, well drained
	¼ teaspoon salt
	Freshly ground pepper
	Cayenne to taste
	1 large clove garlic
	2 tablespoons red wine vinegar
	2 tablespoons lemon juice
	2 tablespoons minced parsley
	Olive oil
For each person:	1 large lemon
	A Kaiser or Vienna roll
	Ice cubes
	A finger bowl

SELECT 4 FULL STALKS OF SEAWEED and place them in a large bowl.
Cover with 2½ quarts of cool water and leave to soak for 10 minutes or
until the seaweed is olive green and fully expanded. Lift out the seaweed
and set aside on a platter. Pour the soaking water into a large pot and
add all the ingredients for the court-bouillon. Bring to a boil, then turn
down the heat, cover the pot, and simmer slowly for 20 minutes.

Return the court-bouillon to a boil and drop in 2 lobsters, head first.
Cover and return to the boil, then immediately reduce to a simmer.
From this point, count 5 minutes for 1-pound lobsters; 6 minutes for
1¼-pound lobsters; 7 minutes for a good 1½-pound beast. Lift out the
lobsters, drain well, and let them cool. Repeat for remaining 2 lobsters.
Save 1 cup of the court-bouillon.

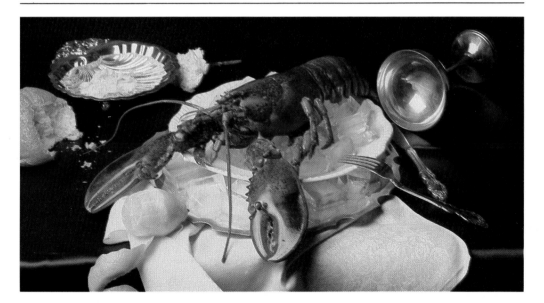

To make the marinade, place the 1 cup of poaching liquid in a small pan and add the shallots. Bring to a boil, then simmer briefly, just until the shallots reach an edible, only slightly crisp texture. Drain and set aside.

Chop the tomatoes coarsely, place them in a pan, and simmer until dry and very thick. Sieve.

Place salt, pepper, cayenne, and garlic in a mortar and crush to a fine paste. Add tomato purée, vinegar, and lemon juice and mix well. Stir in the shallots and parsley, then start beating in olive oil with a fork. Add a good ⅔ cup, then, tasting as you go, add more oil and salt or cayenne as necessary to form a sharp, tasty sauce. Chill the sauce until it thickens somewhat and then taste again for seasoning, as cold tends to obliterate flavor.

With a skewer, punch a neat hole in the carapace (large top shell) of each of the lobsters. Cut out a small ⅓-inch plug of shell, and then open holes in the claws also.

Spoon some of the slightly thickened sauce into each lobster's openings, then refrigerate the lobsters for at least 2 hours. Let the lobsters stand at room temperature for 15 minutes before serving so the sauce can liquify.

To arrange the still lifes, place a stalk of seaweed on each of 4 plates and top with ice cubes. Open a large, white napkin at each place setting and, with the napkin draping over the table's edge, place the lobster dish on top. Let the lobster slightly overhang the dish. Cut 4 long spirals of peel from the lemons and arrange one to the side of each dish. Tip a wine goblet at the upper right. Break a roll open and scatter a few crumbs by it. Place a flowered finger bowl at the top left and another napkin casually hanging over the table's edge, where the napkin usually goes.

Serves 4

Steamed Chicken Suprêmes and Vegetables with Sauce Choron

4 chicken breasts
12 small potatoes, preferably new potatoes
12 small carrots, with tops
8 large, very fresh mushrooms
Lemon juice
4 medium tomatoes, *or* 8 Italian plum tomatoes
Lemon slices
Salt and pepper
Minced fresh herbs (parsley, chives, tarragon, lemon thyme)
Leaves of Savoy Cabbage and/or mustard greens

Note: Shrimp, scallops, or skinless filets of sole can be
substituted for the chicken. Other vegetables like asparagus,
broccoli flowerets, parboiled pearl onions, thickly sliced
zucchini, can also be included.)

BONE AND TRIM THE CHICKEN BREASTS. Slip a finger under the skin to
loosen all attaching membranes and pull the skin away from the flesh.
With a small, sharp knife, cut along the breastbone, then slip the knife
down and along the ribs. Use knife and fingers to pull away the entire

portion of meat. Cut away any fat around the edges, and trim the suprême so that the sides are neat and straight. If the thin, narrow portion of the suprême (the mignon) happens to fall away from the larger portion, press it back under the flesh and it will adhere during cooking.

Peel the potatoes and trim them into even, oval shapes. Parboil in salted water for 5 minutes. Drain well.

Scrape the carrots, and leave 2 inches of green tops attached. Trim the carrots into shortened versions of themselves around 1½ inches long. Tie the greens together. Bring a small pan of salted water to the boil and place in the carrots so that only the orange portions are immersed. Parboil for 5 minutes, then drain.

Cut off the stems from the mushrooms. With a stainless-steel knife, peel the mushrooms by stripping off the outer skin starting at the gill edge. Immediately dip the mushrooms in lemon juice.

Peel the tomatoes by parboiling them briefly. Slip off the skins. Cut whole tomatoes in half and gently press out excess juices.

Place chicken suprêmes in the center of 4 dinner plates. Surround them with bunches of carrots, potatoes, mushrooms, tomatoes, lemon slices, and any other vegetables of choice. Season with salt and pepper and a sprinkling of minced herbs. (The plates can be covered with plastic wrap at this point and refrigerated until needed.)

Place plates in the racks of a Chinese steamer and steam over simmering water for 15 minutes. Using pot holders, lift out the plates and keep them warm. Place leaves of Savoy cabbage or mustard greens in the steamer and let them steam until they turn a vivid green (around 1 minute). Surround the vegetables with a frill of greenery and serve the plates at once. Place a bowl of Sauce Choron on table.   Serves 4

SAUCE CHORON

1 cup dry white wine
1 tablespoon tarragon vinegar
1 tablespoon minced shallots
3 sprigs parsley
2 large fresh tomatoes, *or* 3 canned tomatoes, peeled, seeded,
    coarsely chopped
Good grinding of fresh pepper
3 egg yolks
2 sticks unsalted butter, melted
Pinch of salt
2 teaspoons minced fresh herbs (parsley, chives, a touch of
    tarragon, if possible)

PLACE WINE, VINEGAR, SHALLOTS, PARSLEY, TOMATOES, AND PEPPER in a small, heavy saucepan. Reduce over medium heat to half. Lift out parsley sprigs, then press the remaining contents through a fine sieve, making sure the tomatoes in particular pass into purée. Reduce further to 3 tablespoons of liquid.

Whisk the liquid slowly into the egg yolks. Place the liquid back in the small saucepan and return to very low heat. Start whisking in the butter, first by spoonfuls and then in a slow stream until the sauce mounts and thickens. Remove pan from heat as necessary and do not let it get overhot. When the sauce is firm and thick, add salt to taste and stir in the minced herbs. Serve sauce warm but not hot. Serves 4

BUGS AND BUTTERFLIES

5 tablespoons unsalted butter
⅓ cup sugar
1 egg
¾ cup cake flour, sifted after measure
5 tablespoons ground blanched almonds
A few grains of salt
¼ teaspoon finely grated lemon zest

Frosting and decoration:
1 egg white
Vanilla extract
Confectioners sugar, sieved
Food coloring

Butter and flour for baking trays
Several pieces of light, ⅛-inch-thick Styrofoam
(containers from deli takeouts; smooth tops of egg boxes, etc.)

CREAM THE BUTTER AND SUGAR TOGETHER, then add the egg and beat until the mixture is thick and lemon colored. (An electric mixer works to advantage here.) Stir in the flour, nuts, salt, and lemon zest, and blend well. Cover the dough and set aside in the refrigerator to chill slightly.

Preheat the oven to 350 degrees.

Butter and flour 2 heavy baking sheets. (Rub the sheet with butter, place a solid line of flour at one end, then tip the tray and the flour will coat evenly.)

Draw insect shapes directly on the Styrofoam. The forms should be just slightly smaller than you wish them. Use small scissors to cut out the designs.

Place an insect pattern on the baking sheet. Using water-moistened fingers and a metal spatula, pat and press the dough into the mold and scrape the excess dough off level with the foam. Fill the sheets with designs, then bake them in the oven for 9 or 10 minutes. (Check the oven and turn the trays if certain areas are browning too fast.)

When the cookies are lightly golden at the edges, lift them off the baking sheets and place them at once on racks to cool. (It is possible to lightly bend and prop up the wings of a few butterflies before they cool for more realism.)

When they are cool, frost the cookies with a white undercoat. Whisk the egg white and a few drops of vanilla until frothy. Stir in confectioners sugar until a light frosting is formed. Frost the cookies while they are still on the racks so that all portions can coat evenly. Let dry completely before decorating.

Pour out drops of red, blue, yellow, and green food colorings on a dish. To paint an undercoating, dilute colors with water until they become pale pastels. To make a dark lining color, mix red and green to a pleasing brown and draw on details with a fine brush. To simplify the cookies, make all-white cabbage butterflies, with a few brown details, a frequent butterfly in Flemish paintings. The cookies keep well in a tightly closed container.   Makes around 16 cookies

LEMON POT DE CRÈME

> 5 tablespoons unsalted butter
> ⅓ cup plus 2 tablespoons sugar
> ⅓ cup lemon juice, strained
> 1 large whole egg, separated, plus 2 egg yolks
> 1 teaspoon finely grated lemon zest (only the
>   delicate outer yellow, no white rind)
> Pinch of salt

Optional   Stiffly whipped cream
garnish: Pistachio nuts, finely chopped

PLACE BUTTER, SUGAR, LEMON JUICE, AND 3 EGG YOLKS in a heavy stainless, glass, or enameled saucepan. Place the pan on a trivet in a larger pot containing hot water. Stir constantly with a stainless-steel whisk or wooden spatula over medium heat, until the mixture turns very thick. (It will have about it an almost glazed, gelatinous quality and, when dropped from the stirring utensil, it will form a heavy, unmoving ribbon on the surface of the cream.) At no time should the mixture be allowed to boil.

Remove pan from heat and scrape into a bowl. Stir in the lemon zest and let the custard cool by resting the bottom of the bowl in cool water.

Whip the egg white with a pinch of salt until stiff and glossy. Lightly stir it into the lemon mixture, then fill 4 *pot de crème* pots or small soufflé cups with the mixture. Cover and refrigerate until chilled.

For an optional garnish, pipe a small rosette of whipped cream at the center of each pot, and rim the edge with chopped pistachio nuts.

Makes 4 large portions or 6 smaller ones

FRUIT PLATES

	Lemon juice
	Apples, both yellow and red
	Green and purple grapes
	Bananas
	Strawberries with stems
	Blueberries
	Peaches *or* nectarines *or* papayas
	Mint leaves or other greenery
Optional:	Kiwi fruit
	Bing cherries

HAVE 3 OR 4 SMALL BOWLS OF WATER and lemon juice ready for dipping fruits, particularly apples, bananas, and kiwi, as they are sliced. Work with a stainless-steel knife.

Decide the design of the plates beforehand or copy the photograph (page 7). The Lemon Pot de Crème can either be placed in the middle of the plate or off the plate and to the side if a larger fruit plate is to be used as an entire luncheon dish.

Slice the apples so that a good portion of peel is apparent on each slice. Dip the slices in lemon juice. Peaches and kiwi can also be sliced ahead and dipped in juices. The plates can be prepared 1 hour ahead (except for the banana and apple additions), and kept covered tightly with plastic wrap in the refrigerator.

Use apple slices carefully fanned to represent tulips. Grapes can be sliced and aligned to suggest budding branches. Offset the plate's border by uneven arrangements that extend to and above the rim, and let greenery trail off the edge. Two or 3 strawberries or cherries should be at the side of the plate as if they have fallen off.

A butterfly can be propped at the side of the Pot de Crème by inserting a toothpick and letting the cookie rest against it. (In the summer, a scoop of pineapple sherbet, molded with a spoon to look vaguely like a flower at the center of the plate, is faster and easier to prepare and can substitute for the Pot de Crème.)

Cotán, *Quince, Cabbage, Melon and Cucumber*. San Diego Museum of Art

A Trompe L'Oeil Dinner

The Inspiration

. . . the illusionist creations of fool-the-eye duplicity that so often take food as their inspiration.

Trompe l'oeil paintings are closely related to still lifes in that they copy a formally arranged set of objects. But whereas the Flemish masters had an interest in capturing the exact tones and textures of fruits and flowers, there was little or no suggestion that those fruits and flowers were anything but painstaking oil paint upon a canvas meant to be framed.

When there is a conscious effort to fool the eye into believing that the shadowed, life-sized bowl of flowers or fruits is actually sitting on an accessible shelf, when the viewer reaches out to touch the marble shelf and finds it only painted canvas, then the artist has succeeded in trompe l'oeil deception.

The earliest paintings of the genre are found in ancient Greek and Roman buildings. Pliny the Elder recorded that Roman painters could execute bunches of grapes so realistically that small birds flew down from the heavens to peck at them. Flat walls were decorated with painted

A Trompe
L'Oeil
Dinner

niches and illusionary doorways, and on one famous mosaic floor, called *The Unswept Room*, an artist placed bones and nutshells, fruit pits and fish skeletons, all faithfully rendered in chipped marble.

In seventeenth- and eighteenth-century England and France, porcelain manufacturers created countless reproductions of vegetables. There were elegant tureens in the shapes of cabbages and plates affixed with ceramic nuts, cheeses, asparagus spears, and olives. The aristocracy delighted in setting them among the real side dishes as a banquet joke. And when eighteenth-century England faced a severe flour shortage, and bakers were by law not allowed to enclose their meat pies in pastry, the firm of Wedgwood created pâté molds of pastry-colored clay which at least fooled the eye, if not the stomach, of the English consumer.

An entire trompe l'oeil meal is an amusing way in which to test one's ingenuity and creativity. Desserts are easy to imagine, for baked goods and pastries lend themselves to being disguised in a variety of forms. It is more difficult to find a main course that can pass itself off as something else. The most reasonable thing to do is to offer a meat or vegetable that suggests another. I, for one, think it most disquieting to bite into an apple and find a meatball, and vice versa. Above all, a trompe l'oeil meal should remain appetizing and edible, for though the foolish eye may be quickly and happily taken, the more knowing mouth resents deception.

Setting the Scene

Note that this menu is expandable and could easily feed a large crowd. The cake can be doubled into a whole "melon," and most of the other recipes suggest a per-person formula. Homemade chicken stock is called for in two recipes; prepare one large batch the day before, chill it, and lift off the fat.

Have the display of crudités arranged in the kitchen or living room and waiting to accompany any predinner drinks. Set the dining table with a large trompe l'oeil display as a centerpiece. (This could be silk flowers; papier-mâché vegetables, an assortment of basket "nests" containing wild grasses, ostrich eggs, walnut "eggs," etc., or whatever one can devise.)

Serve Eggs in a Nest and Braised "Chops" in formal courses dished up and carried in from the kitchen. Clear the table and remove the centerpiece, also.

Place the "Watermelon" Cake on a large serving tray, add a chef's knife, and put the melon in the middle of the table. (A real cantaloupe or two might join it.) Serve everyone an ice cream "avocado" on a large dessert plate, and let the guests cut their own slices of cake and serve themselves from an assortment of sauces and toppings. Serve coffee and "caviar" separately after the dessert.

If you have any control over the lighting, direct a strong, overhead source of illumination diagonally from right to left at the center of the table which will cause the deep shadowing chiaroscuro that artists use to give painted objects verisimilitude.

For music, listen to classics with a humorous twist, such as Hayden's *Surprise Symphony* or Stephane Grappelli's *Brandenburg Boogie*.

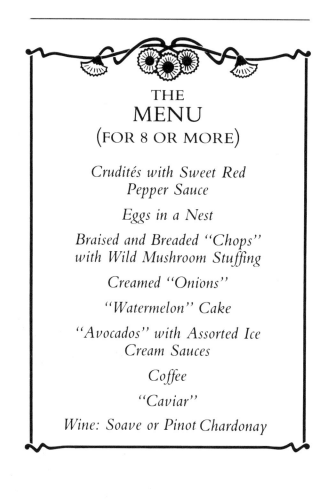

THE
MENU
(FOR 8 OR MORE)

*Crudités with Sweet Red
Pepper Sauce*

Eggs in a Nest

*Braised and Breaded "Chops"
with Wild Mushroom Stuffing*

Creamed "Onions"

"Watermelon" Cake

*"Avocados" with Assorted Ice
Cream Sauces*

Coffee

"Caviar"

Wine: Soave or Pinot Chardonay

Crudités with Sweet Red Pepper Sauce

Sauce:

5 large, sweet red peppers
4 large ripe tomatoes, *or* the equivalent of
    canned tomatoes, pressed dry
2 cloves garlic, minced
3½ ounces blanched almonds, ground
Salt, freshly ground pepper
Cayenne
½ cup mayonnaise
Red wine vinegar
Olive oil

Crudités:

An assortment of

Carrots, scraped, with 2 inches of tops left on
Italian plum tomatoes
Tender fennel hearts, halved
Celery hearts, halved
Green and red peppers, halved and seeded
Whole pretty bunches of radishes, washed and
    trimmed
Large black or green olives
Small, parboiled artichokes
Cauliflower flowerets
Broccoli flowerets
Olive oil
A few life-sized ceramic vegetables

PEEL THE PEPPERS for the sauce by placing them on a grill or under a broiler until the skins are blistered and blackened on all sides. When they are cool enough to handle, peel and seed them. (Save all juices that collect; they are a marvelous addition to vinaigrette dressings.)

Bring a pan of water to a boil, and place in the fresh tomatoes for 1 minute. Strain out and peel. Cut the tomatoes in half across their width and squeeze each portion until all seeds and juice are expelled. Chop coarsely, take the tomatoes up by handfuls, and squeeze again until very dry.

Place peppers, tomatoes, garlic, almonds, seasonings, mayonnaise, and 1 tablespoon vinegar in a food processor or blender. Purée, slowly adding a bit of oil until the mixture is the consistency of a thick dipping sauce. Taste for seasoning. There should be a distinctly hot taste. Add more vinegar or salt if necessary. Refrigerate for at least 3 hours before serving. Makes about 3 cups.

To serve, select an assortment of pretty plates. Place the vegetables on the plates and include at random the trompe l'oeil vegetables. Dip a finger in olive oil and lightly glaze the real vegetables so that they more nearly resemble their ceramic counterparts. Put the sauce in their midst, and place knives nearby. (In our picture, the fennel, artichokes, figs, melon, and 1 green pepper are fake.)   Serves 8

EGGS IN A NEST

The following poached eggs are formed in an 8-indentation Wilton cake pan that is meant to mold cakes in the shape of Easter eggs. The pan is available in most hobby and craft stores. Plain poached eggs can be substituted, of course.

20 ounces fresh spinach, rinsed and stemmed
1 stick plus 1 tablespoon unsalted butter
Salt, pepper, nutmeg
1 quart peanut oil
2 ounces bean threads (Oriental mung bean noodles)
3 tablespoons flour
5 cups homemade chicken stock, fat free
14 eggs plus 2 egg whites

PLACE THE SPINACH IN A LARGE PAN, salt it lightly, and cook it in only the water clinging to the leaves. When just tender and still bright in color, turn the spinach into a colander and rinse under a gentle stream of cool water. Press out all liquid from the mass and chop the spinach coarsely.

Heat 4 tablespoons of butter in a frying pan and let it turn a dark nut brown. Immediately add the spinach and stir until the butter is incorporated. Season with salt, pepper, and 3 or 4 scrapings of nutmeg. Cover and hold until needed.

Heat the peanut oil in a large, deep-sided pan. When very hot, test the oil by dropping in a strand of bean thread. If it immediately sizzles, sending out a foam of fine breaking bubbles, the oil is hot enough. Break the bean threads into short sections and fry in several batches to a golden brown. (Do not overcrowd the pan.) Strain out, and drain on absorbent paper. (These can be stored in an airtight container and reheated, along with the spinach, in a warming oven when needed.)

Prepare a sauce by melting 3 tablespoons of butter in a heavy saucepan. Add 3 tablespoons of flour and stir over low heat for 2 minutes. Whisk in 4 cups of chicken stock and a scraping of nutmeg. Bring to a boil, then let the sauce simmer for 20 minutes over very low heat. Carefully lift off the skin that has formed over the sauce and discard.

Separate 6 of the eggs. Place 6 yolks and the remaining cup of stock in a bowl and stir. Slowly whisk in the hot sauce, then return the entire mixture to the heat. Continue cooking, stirring all the while, until the sauce thickens and coats a spoon. Strain, adjust seasoning, and place in a clean saucepan. Melt 2 tablespoons of butter and pour over the sauce so no surface film can form.

Poach the remaining whole eggs. If using a mold, coat each indentation with a thick, generous layer of butter. Into each indentation put 2 whites and then try to center a yolk. Salt lightly. Bring 1 inch of water in a roasting pan to a simmer on top of the stove. Set in the pan containing the eggs and cover the pan lightly with a sheet of buttered foil. Poach for around 10 minutes or until the whites are firmly set but the yolks are still soft.

While the eggs are poaching, arrange the nests. Divide the warmed spinach among 8 bowls. Gently reheat the sauce, whisking in the butter on the surface. Using a soup spoon, lift out each egg from the mold and place it on top of the spinach. Surround with crisp bean threads. Serve and immediately let the host ladle the rich egg sauce over each serving. (Note: This is a glorified version of *Oeufs Florentine*.)   Serves 8

Braised and Breaded "Chops" with Wild Mushroom Stuffing

8 whole chicken legs
½ cup flour
Salt and pepper
5 tablespoons unsalted butter
7 tablespoons olive oil
½ cup dry white wine
2 cups defatted chicken stock
1 egg lightly beaten with 2 tablespoons milk
1½ cups fine, dry bread crumbs (passed through a sieve)

Mirepoix:
2 tablespoons unsalted butter
2 tablespoons olive oil
2 medium-large onions, chopped
1 clove garlic, minced
3 carrots, scraped and chopped
1 bay leaf
1 tablespoon minced parsley
½ teaspoon mixed dried herbs (thyme, oregano, savory)
Salt and pepper

Stuffing:
2 ounces dried mushrooms (morels, cèpes, girolles, *or* substitute ½ dried Chinese black mushrooms and ½ fresh mushrooms)
1 tablespoon unsalted butter
1 garlic clove, minced
2 teaspoons parsley, finely minced
¼ teaspoon grated lemon zest
Salt and pepper

A trussing needle
· Thin kitchen string
Cutlet Frills (see Note)

TO PREPARE THE MIREPOIX BRAISING BED, heat butter and oil in a large frying pan, then add the onions and garlic. Cover and cook over low heat until the onions are just tender but not browned. Remove and reserve ¼ cup of onions. To those remaining in the pan, add carrots, bay leaf, herbs, and seasonings. Continue cooking, covered, for another 20 minutes. Set aside.

To prepare the stuffing, soak the dried mushrooms in cool, covering water for 30 minutes. Cut off any tough portions of stems and gently squeeze the mushrooms to remove excess liquid. Chop finely. Melt butter in a frying pan and add the reserved ¼ cup of onions and the minced garlic. Sauté briefly, then add mushrooms, parsley, lemon zest, and seasonings. Stir rapidly over brisk heat for 1 minute. Purée the mushroom mixture and set aside.

Preheat the oven to 350 degrees.

Bone the chicken legs. With a small, sharp knife, begin at the top of the thigh and run the knife around the large knob of bone, severing in the process all tendons and ligaments; then scrape the knife down the length of bone toward the drumstick joint. Again, cut around the joint and twist off the thigh bone. Continue scraping down the drumstick until the bone length is half exposed. Cut the bone off with the sharp blow of a cleaver and remove any loose shards that might have broken off in the process. Leave the remaining end of bone in the leg.

Stuff a portion of the mushroom paste down into each leg. Thread a trussing needle with string and thoroughly sew up the thigh opening. Season flour with salt, place it in a paper bag, and add the chicken legs. Gently shake the bag until the chicken is evenly coated with flour. Heat 2 tablespoons of butter and 4 tablespoons of oil in a frying pan and quickly brown the sides of each leg.

Spread the mirepoix in a roasting pan and place the browned legs on top. Pour off the fat from the frying pan and deglaze with the wine, scraping up all savory caramelizations in the process. Pour the deglazing juices and chicken stock over the legs. Cover the pan and bake in an oven for 40 minutes.

Remove the legs from the pan, place them on a platter, and immediately cover them with another flat platter. Place 4 to 5 pounds of canned goods on top and let cool to room temperature before refrigerating overnight, weights and all. Strain the contents of the braising pan and refrigerate them, also. When the juices are cold, lift off the solidified fat on the surface.

Let the chicken legs come to room temperature 1 hour before guests arrive. Pat them dry with paper toweling, and roll them lightly in additional salted flour and then in beaten egg and milk. Place the legs in a bowl of bread crumbs and coat them evenly. Place the legs on cake racks as they are finished, and allow them to dry for at least 20 minutes (or they can be covered lightly with foil and kept an hour or so).

Heat 3 tablespoons of butter and 3 tablespoons of oil in a large pan and fry the chicken legs until crisp and brown. Dress the bone ends with cutlet frills. The braising juices should be reduced by one-third and served as a light, accompanying flavoring essence. Serves 8

PAPER FRILLS

*To make a cutlet frill, cut 8 4 × 5-inch
rectangles of kitchen parchment or plain white
paper. Fold them in half lengthwise, then cut the
folded edge into a fine fringe 1 inch long. Open up
the paper and fold it in half again lengthwise but in
the opposite direction, so that the fringe can open
and expand. Curl up the frill to fit the size of the
chicken bones and glue the ends (holding them with
a paper clip until dry) or, less elegantly, tape them.
Slip the frills over the bones just before serving.*

CREAMED "ONIONS"

8 large radishes per person, *or* 8 rounds of turnip
    cut out with a melon baller
Heavy cream
Salt and pepper

IF USING RADISHES, peel off the red exteriors. Bring a pan of salted
water to the boil and parboil either radishes or turnips until just tender.
Drain well.

Place the vegetables back in a pan and cover with heavy cream. Heat
and reduce the cream until it has thickened to the consistency of a
medium white sauce. Season with salt and pepper and serve. (Either
vegetable will resemble creamed onions when cooked.)

The following recipe makes half a watermelon. To make a whole
melon, as is pictured on page 29, make 2 batches of the recipe. (Do *not*
simply double the recipe, as most home equipment cannot handle the
volume of batter that this will produce.) Place 1 cake on top of the other
as soon as it comes from the oven, and the escaping moisture will act to
fuse the halves together. Cut a slice from the melon with a serrated knife,
and trim and slightly flatten 2 sides of the round to suggest a more ovoid
shape.　　　　The double-halved whole melon serves 20 to 24 people

"Watermelon" Cake

8 eggs plus 2 egg yolks
1⅓ cups granulated sugar
2 teaspoons vanilla extract
1 teaspoon finely grated zest of lemon
2 cups all-purpose flour, sifted
5 tablespoons unsalted butter, melted

Softened, unsalted butter for baking pan and
coating cake

Frosting:

2 tablespoons unsalted butter, melted
1 teaspoon vanilla extract
2 tablespoons heavy cream
Sieved confectioners sugar

Red, yellow, green, and blue food coloring
Flat licorice or black jelly beans

GENEROUSLY BUTTER AND FLOUR a 5-quart stainless-steel bowl. Preheat the oven to 350 degrees.

Combine eggs, egg yolks, sugar, vanilla, and lemon zest in the metal bowl of a mixer or in a large, stainless-steel mixing bowl. Place the bowl directly over very low heat, and, with your hand, combine eggs and sugar until the mixture is warm and you can feel that the sugar granules are dissolved. Remove from the heat and beat with a mixer until the eggs are thick and have tripled in volume. Drop some of the mixture on top of the batter and note the amount of time it takes for the ribbon to dissolve back into the mass. A professional baker would wish the ribbon to hold 3 seconds.

Gently, rapidly, fold the flour into the eggs in 3 or 4 portions. (A hand with fingers stiffly spread does the most thorough job, for it can feel any pockets of unmixed flour.) Sprinkle on the melted butter and fold it in, also.

Scrape the batter into the greased baking bowl, set the bowl on a cookie sheet to help the even distribution of heat during baking, and place in the oven. Bake for around 1 hour, covering the cake at the end of that time if it threatens to over-brown. The cake should come away from the sides of the bowl, and the center should feel and be firm when pressed with a finger.

Remove cake from oven, let it cool for 5 minutes, then turn it out and set it broad surface up until completely cool. Trim away any over-crisp edges. Brush away loose crumbs from the surface and place the cake on a plate.

To facilitate frosting, spread a thin layer of very soft butter over the entire surface of the cake, and place in a freezer until hard. This will help smooth the surface that is to be frosted and encourage the frosting to set quickly as it is applied.

Mix together the melted butter, vanilla, and cream. Sieve in confectioners sugar until the consistency is medium-firm. Bring the cake from the freezer and, working rapidly, frost a layer of white around the rim of the cake to suggest the rind of watermelon. Spoon some of the frosting into a bowl and tint it pink. Add a drop of yellow food coloring. Frost the pink interior of the melon. Tint the remaining frosting green and add drops of blue and yellow until the shade is grasslike in color. Frost the melon's exterior. Leave the melon to harden and dry for a good 1½ hours.

For the final realistic touches, mix a dark blue-green shade of food coloring and paint on melon stripes over the green shell. Mix a shade of deep peach (red and yellow), and, using a clean cloth, wipe it rapidly over the pink and white portions of the interior for details and highlights. The center should be the darkest pink. When these colors have dried, affix watermelon "seeds." Cut licorice or jelly beans into small seeds and insert them into the pink melon flesh. Baked as a half melon.

Serves 10 to 12 people

ICE CREAM "AVOCADOS"

1 large avocado half shell per person
Pale, peach-colored ice cream of choice (do not use sherbet)
Light chocolate or coffee ice cream

SAVE AVOCADO SHELLS over a period of time. As each half shell is emptied, scrape it well to remove adhering flesh and wipe out the interior. Immediately freeze the shell, then store it in a freezer bag until enough have been collected.

One day before the avocados are needed, soften the peach-colored ice cream by stirring it with a heavy spoon. Spoon into the shells (do not worry about a smooth edge). Let freeze hard, then cut off the ice cream level with the shell. Make a large, scooped indentation in the avocados with a spoon. In half of them, place a rounded mound of chocolate ice cream to represent the seed. Freeze very hard.

With the cake and ice cream, serve an assortment of sauces: Chocolate (page 103); caramel; a sweetened, sieved purée of raspberries; or any others of choice.

"Caviar"

Rock crystal sugar
1 jar mint candy "caviar" (see Note)
Candy lemon slices (jelly candies)

FILL A GLASS BOWL with rock crystal sugar and nestle the whole jar of candy caviar in the center. Cut lemon slices half way through and slip them over the edge of the "ice" container. Serve the mints with coffee.

Note: Candy caviar is available by mail order from A Southern Season, Chapel Hill, North Carolina 27514.

A
SURREAL
FANTASY

The Inspiration

. . . the surreal food fantasies of Dali, Magritte, and Marinetti.

If the trompe l'oeil artist hopes to deceive the eye, the surrealist would take matters a few steps farther and try to trick the very mind into a willing suspension of its disbelief. In the strange world of the surreal, the artist looks with fresh, frequently perverse eyes upon the normal experience of life, the common objects of our daily concern, and then twists that ordinariness into a strange suggestion of otherness, of something visionary, unforeseen, absurd. When we view the paintings, it is always with a slight and wondrous shock, as if some fragmented half-dream had suddenly, preposterously, sprung to life before us.

Because food is such a known universal, because it faces us so benignly three times a day at table, surrealist painters often turn to cuisine for subject matter. René Magritte in particular loved to suggest the bizarre and to worry us with the sinister in the most common of foodstuffs. In his paintings a single green apple expands to fill an entire room (can it

Magritte, *Portrait.* Collection, ~~u~~m of Modern Art, New York. Gift of ~~a~~te Tanguy. 1935, Oil on canvas, ~~x~~ 19⅞"

A
Surreal
Fantasy

explode? will detonating juice and pips annihilate us all?). A masked grapefruit lurks in the shadows (might it suddenly roll forward and demand our money or our life?). A huge *baguette* hovers in a starry sky (if the buoyancy above us ends, will bread bolt down and crush us with apocalyptic crumbs?).

In the paintings of Salvador Dali, we also see a distorted version of common foodstuffs. Dali, like so many artists, was particularly interested in primal eggs, and they drape with frequency about his paintings, as do his famous limp watches which melt like ripe Camembert upon the canvas. In his autobiography, Dali tells us that as a child he wished to be a cook. Perhaps it was a desirable loss to the *metier*, for strange indeed would have been his confections. Was it possible, he wondered, to construct a Venus de Milo entirely of eggs, to pour the whites into a shapely mold, poach them, then force in the yolks through a tubing system? When the lady solidified you could salt her and devour her sensual nourishment with a spoon. Or why not paint the flourescent portrait of a saint on chick peas. Spill down the peas from a great height, shine a light on them, and form an edible religious icon before the very eyes. As a cook, Dali would also have been limited by his rather exacting choice in foods. Spinach and lettuce were to be abhorred, for instance, because of their "sordid, amorphous character." Better that foods have well-defined shapes with bones and skeletons throughout that could be crunched

between the teeth. (And Dali would bite into anything . . . chests, butterflies, onions, glass, hats . . . to sense and know its soul.)

If the surreal artist seems a poseur at times, it is because his intended wish is to jolt the staid bourgeois from their lethargy. In 1932, the Italian poet Filippo Marinetti published a book entitled *La Cucina Futurista*. In it, he railed against the consumption of pasta in his native land, a substance he felt was brutalizing the Italian populace and inducing it to sloth and pessimism. He, like Dali, then proceeded to astound the public with peculiar dishes meant to shock and titillate. There were sausages poached in black coffee flavored with eau de cologne, and odd aphrodisiacs featuring fruit juices, caviar, and hot pepper. In a throwback to earlier Roman banquets, he declared that during futurist meals the diners should be sprayed with perfume and that they should eat with one hand while stroking a sensuous material with the other.

The surreal meal may not always be practical or feasible, but the imagination at work behind the concept is fascinating. "I know what I eat" says Dali at the beginning of his autobiography, but even he admits, "I do not know what I do."

Setting the Scene

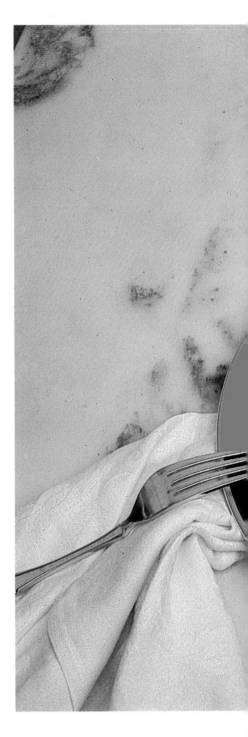

The true surreal meal is, above all, a joke, and I do not seriously propose to offer one here. Rather, it might be considered an extension of the trompe l'oeil concept and, for an April Fool's Day dinner, one might turn particularly to Magritte for many ideas for table settings.

In a centerpiece, a fork plunges into something nonedible. Spoons appear in odd, not-to-be-expected places. Objects gathered within a frame laid at the center of the table bear strange relationships to each other. Instead of flowers, arrange a shaving brush, a shoe, a comb, an apple. Instead of candles upright in their sticks, try turning them into the wormlike forms that creep across the sand in Magritte's painting *Meditation*. (Purchase 15-inch candles, put them in a roasting pan, and place them in a warm oven. When the candles soften, carefully bend the narrow, wick end into the tail and body of a snake. Prop the thick end of the candle upright against a tumbler. When the candle hardens, cut off the wick and scrape the wax away from the wide, upright end of the candle to expose the wick which can then be lit.)

Purchase some inexpensive flatware and have a tinsmith stretch apart the tines of the forks, curl up the knife blades, and bend the spoons abruptly; then serve pasta, Marinetti be damned.

Place a peacock feather in everyone's wine glass. Serve oyster shells with odd, unexpected foods in them. Serve Marinetti's Divorced Eggs (a purée of potatoes holding the yolk of a hard-boiled egg; the white of the boiled egg holding a purée of carrots). Offer up plates of mundane peas, potatoes, and slices of ham, but in the ham bone's place, put a bloodshot paper eye to rivet the diner.

Using acrylic paints, paint a sky-blue tablecloth with white clouds so that the whole meal seems to levitate above the surface of the table.

Exalt a cheese dome on a pedestal but place under the dome only the painting of a cheese. Let the real object rest humbly on the table.

For dessert, set a scene with ominous masked grapefruits looking on while a stabbed citrus victim, bleeding raspberry purée, lies helplessly nearby.

Dramatizing a Scene

A
Rousseau
Jungle
Feast

The Inspiration

. . . the fanciful paintings of Henri Rousseau, the gentle, childlike artist whose visions of foreign worlds so graphically show us that jungles of the imagination are more vivid and more fascinating than any in reality.

Rousseau, as far as anyone can tell, never visited a jungle, but he used to sit for hours sketching leaves and plants in the botanical gardens of Paris. He visited zoos, staring at the monkeys and great cats, and then returned to his poor studio to assiduously transcribe his tropical visions. Reeds and poplar leaves, Egyptian lotus flowers and spiked white blossoms from a yucca are juxtaposed on canvas in a fashion so orderly that it almost looks as if someone had taken a comb to the jungle. Woven into the foliage are myriad odd, startling beasts, with a hint of a snake's tail here, the eyes of a bird of prey glimpsed high in a tree there. Sometimes, an observer recorded, Rousseau would be so frightened as he painted his glaring

A Rousseau
Jungle
Feast

creations that he would fling open a
window and gulp the cool, fresh air to
recompose himself. (I did indeed once live
in the jungles of Africa for two years, and
dense and green they were, with a mess of
vines and creepers ready to entangle one,
but never did one actually see bright
flowers floating there or any beasts,
though deep in the night you could hear
their calls.)

Rousseau's many paintings, with their
monkeys at play among the fruits and
flowers, inspired one of my first
Entertainments, for as I gazed at the
paintings, the vegetation transformed itself
so readily into vegetable matter. The
plump olive spikes behind the monkeys
looked like asparagus; the reedlike grass at
the picture's foreground might easily be
green beans; carrots were fruit falling in
profusion from the trees; and egg-white
flowers sprang from the jungle floor.
There, *voilà*, were all the makings of a
salad.

To follow a salad first course, the main
course presents a two-in-one dish of
poultry with a choice of couscous or rice
and North African Onion Sauce or West
African Groundnut Sauce. (True jungle
food is, in reality, also less exotic than one
might imagine. The indigenous people
where I lived dined, as I recall, mainly on
rice and dried fish, or on viscous
substances made from thoroughly pounded
yams and cassava roots, and aptly named
fufu and *dumboy*. Sometimes, however, if
you gave a young boy a quarter, he would
cut and core the heart from a young palm

tree, or fetch you five butterpear avocadoes large as grapefruits, or a whole cluster of bananas each as big as a man's thumb and sweet as sugar, which Rousseau's monkeys would love to have devoured.)

Setting the Scene

The table can be placed either outdoors or in a dining room laden with greenery. To lessen expenses, cuttings of bamboo can be stabilized in large flowerpots, or oversized bouquets of tree or shrubbery branches could provide part of the landscape. Choose a tablecloth of palest apple green or a vivid blue, such as Rousseau painted his sky. Make a large centerpiece of greenery. The easiest to come by is a piece of florist's Oasis pierced with a multitude of leaves (ivy and cut branches of jade plant and asparagus fern from a florist). Place the centerpiece on a sheet of aluminum foil, moisten the oasis, and the greens will remain fresh throughout the meal. A small beast should repose at and peer out from the center (in the accompanying picture, a Stratfordshire lion does the honors, but a child's stuffed animal could be just as effective). Surround the beast with several yellow-bordered snake plants, spiked aloes, or bromeliads in bloom.

Place bamboo mats under the plates. Fold large napkins into quarters and roll them up. Slip bamboo or tortoise napkin rings over the lengths and tuck a sprig of ivy into the holders. (Everywhere there should be the sense of encroaching foliage.)

Have the salad plates at each place setting when guests are called to table. The main course should be set up buffet style after the salad and, after the guests help themselves, the desserts—all assembled ahead and refrigerated—can be formally served.

For an added touch of fantasy, rent a gaudy parrot from a pet store. It will stand on its head, flirt with the guests, screech at appropriate moments, and generally charm and enliven the occasion.

THE
MENU
(FOR 8 TO 10)

Bread Beasts

Exotic Salad

*Braised Rock Cornish Game
Hens à la Crapaudine*

West African Groundnut Sauce

North African Onion Sauce

Check Rice

Couscous

Oranges Bavarian

Wine: a Rosé

51

Bread Beasts

MAKE 1 RECIPE OF PLAIN FRESH BREAD (see page 142). Let the dough rise once, then punch it down and immediately start forming animals. Roll out the dough ¾ inch thick. Cut a fat oval. Cut 2 arms along the edge and fold them into the center. Cut indentations at the neck and push a bearlike face into shape. Pinch up the ears and place a ball of dough in the nose position. Make large holes with a skewer for the eyes and mouth, and attach 2 plump knees and legs to the main body. (The animal should be about 5 inches long before baking.) Continue to make more beasts until dough is used up.

Brush the beasts overall with a glaze of egg yolk beaten with a tablespoon of water. Leave to rise briefly, then bake in a 375-degree oven for around 20 minutes or until nicely golden. (Protect ears and nose from overbrowning with aluminum foil if necessary.)   Yields 10 to 12 beasts

Exotic Salad

For each salad: Few slices of carrot
6 to 8 asparagus spears
Large handful of green beans
2 strips of sweet red pepper or tomato
½ hard-boiled egg
Watercress
1 bread beast
Oil and vinegar dressing, with fresh herbs and a
    hint of garlic

PLUNGE THE CARROT SLICES into boiling water, then remove them immediately and refresh under cold water.

Salt the water and bring it back to a boil. Break the asparagus so that you have 3-inch tips. (The bottom lengths can be peeled and retained for soup.) Tie the asparagus into bunches and cook it until it reaches a pleasantly crisp *al dente*. Refresh under cold water.

Cut the green beans into thin lengths or slice them on a french-cut bean slicer. Parboil the beans in boiling, salted water very briefly. They should remain bright green and slightly crunchy. Drain and refresh under cold water to set the color. Have all vegetables chilled and thoroughly dried.

To assemble the salads, place a bread beast slightly off center on a large dinner plate. Arrange tall asparagus at either side. Plant a thicket of green-bean "grass" over the lower portion of the plate. Cut the pepper or tomato into small, tulip-shaped pieces and build a tall red flower. Cut egg white into petals and form a white flower with a portion of yolk at its center. Tuck some watercress under the beans at the left side of the plate (forget the border and let the "tree" overhang the edge), and place carrot "oranges" randomly about in the tree and 1 in the clutch of each bread beast.

The host or hostess should lead in the eating of the salad. Remove the beast and slice the beans, asparagus, and watercress. Pass a sauceboat of dressing and let each guest serve himself, then toss his own salad on his plate.

BRAISED ROCK CORNISH HENS À LA CRAPAUDINE

8 to 10 Rock Cornish game hens
3 tablespoons butter
3 tablespoons olive or peanut oil
2 large onions, chopped
3 large carrots, diced
¼ cup minced fresh parsley
2 tablespoons mixed dried herbs (thyme, oregano, savory)
1 bay leaf
Salt and pepper
3 cups chicken stock, boiling
Melted butter for basting
Pitted black olives

A trussing needle and string

SALT THE INTERIORS OF THE BIRDS. Cut the game hens *à la crapaudine* (like toads). Place hen on its back. With a sharp chef's knife, cut directly into the breast at its highest midpoint and, slanting the cut toward the shoulder joint, continue to cut to just short of the shoulder bone. This loosened flap of breast meat will become the "head" of the toad. Turn the bird over and lift and fold the "head" back (the loose skin at the neck should now rest on the back of the bird). Fold and tuck the wings under. With the flat of your hand, press down on the bird until all resisting bones crack and the hen is lying flat. With a length of string, tie the drumsticks together, then run the string over and around the hind quarter 2 or 3 times so they remain compact. Thread a trussing needle with kitchen string and, with 4 or 5 stitches, sew the loose skin on the "head" to the back.

When all the birds are prepared, heat butter and oil in a large sauté pan (use 2 pans if necessary), and lightly brown the tops of the birds (around 10 minutes). Remove birds to a platter and, in the remaining oil, cook onions, carrots, parsley, dried herbs and bay leaf until limp, scraping up in the process all the caramelized juices from frying so as not to waste this good flavor.

Preheat the oven to 375 degrees.

In a large roasting pan, spread the vegetables and place the birds on top. Season generously. Pour the hot stock over the birds and cover well with aluminum foil. Place the birds in the oven and bake for 30 minutes. Remove the foil and baste the birds with melted butter and pan juices.

Allow the birds another 15 to 20 minutes to turn a handsome golden brown.

Remove the "toads" and pull out the trussing strings. Place birds around the edge of the serving dish heaped with couscous and rice. Cut 2 rounds of black olive and place them on the top of each toad's head for eyes.

The braising juices can be used to dilute the Groundnut Sauce if they are needed.

West African Groundnut Sauce

½ cup peanut oil (or palm oil, if available)
3 large onions, chopped
5 large tomatoes, peeled and puréed, *or* 1 28-ounce can
    tomatoes, drained
1 cup thick, homemade tomato sauce
2 large cloves garlic, minced
½ teaspoon ground ginger
2 hot chili peppers (whole)
1 teaspoon cayenne, or to taste
Salt and pepper
4 cups boiling water or chicken stock
1 cup peanut butter mixed with 2 cups stock
1 pound okra, sliced
1½ cups coarsely chopped huskless peanuts

HEAT THE PEANUT OIL in a large sauté pan and cook the onions over low heat until they are soft. Add all the remaining ingredients and simmer, covered, for 1 hour. Stir from time to time. Taste carefully for seasoning. If need be, the sauce can be diluted with some of the braising juices from the hens. Remove the chili peppers before serving. This sauce should be distinctly hot, and it is meant to top Check Rice. Can be done ahead and reheated.   Serves 8 to 10

NORTH AFRICAN ONION SAUCE

5 pounds white or yellow onions, sliced thin
6 tablespoons butter
4 apples, diced
4 cups chicken stock
1 cup golden raisins
1 cup dark raisins
3 cloves garlic, minced
½ teaspoon powdered saffron
1 teaspoon turmeric
1 teaspoon ground ginger
⅔ cup sugar
1 teaspoon cinnamon
Salt and pepper

COOK THE ONIONS in the butter over gentle heat until they just begin to turn golden. Add all the remaining ingredients and simmer, covered, for 50 minutes. Uncover and continue to cook until the onions appear glazed and are not overly liquid. Can be done ahead and reheated.

Serves 8 to 10

CHECK RICE

1 small bowl of fresh, young hibiscus leaves, or 8 to 10 turnip
    greens, potato greens, or collards
¼ teaspoon baking soda
3 cups long-grain rice
Salt
3 to 4 tablespoons palm oil or butter

WASH AND STEM THE GREENS. Cut them into thin shreds (chiffonade) and place them, with only the water clinging to the leaves, in a pot. Add baking soda and cook over gentle heat, stirring all the while, until the greens are cooked and dry.

Cook the rice in 6 cups of salted water. Run a knife through the greens to finely chop them. Stir greens into the rice and flavor the rice with palm oil or butter.

Note: Palm oil is sometimes available in specialty stores carrying Caribbean foods. It is a delicious, deep orange oil that is distinctive in flavor. Check the oil carefully before purchase to ensure that it is fresh.

COUSCOUS

4 cups couscous (bulgur wheat)
Salt
½ cup minced parsley

FIRST MOISTEN AND SWELL THE GRAIN. Place the grain in a large sieve and let cool water run over the wheat. Stir with your hand for 5 minutes, then drain well. Spread the grain out (preferably in a large paella dish), and let sit for 15 minutes, then gently rake through the mass with your fingers.

Steam the grain for 20 minutes. (Use a *couscousiere*, or place the grain in a "bowl" of heavy foil which has been perforated with small holes. Place this foil on a rack in a deep pot with water underneath.) Do not cover.

Spread the grain onto a large dish, sprinkle with a bit of water and salt, then rake through the grain with oiled fingers. Let rest for 15 minutes (or longer if protected with a damp towel). Twenty minutes before needed, steam again for a final 20 minutes. To assemble the grains, mound up the rice and couscous on a large platter. Divide the grains with a band of minced parsley.

ORANGES BAVARIAN

11 very large oranges
4 lumps sugar
1¾ cups milk
Juice of 1 lemon
⅓ cup sugar
6 egg yolks
2 tablespoons (2 envelopes) unflavored gelatine, softened in 2
     tablespoons water
1 tablespoon Grand Marnier
1¾ cups heavy cream
1 quart fresh raspberries, *or* 2 packages frozen raspberries,
     thawed
Sugar for sweetening
8 unblanched, whole almonds per person

WITH A SMALL, SHARP KNIFE, cut caps from 10 oranges. Inserting the knife half way through the orange at the top of the fruit, cut at an angle, then continue making cuts at zigzag angles so that the cap has 5 or 6 points. Lift and twist off the cap. Clean out the flesh and juice from the orange with a spoon. The bottom portion will serve as a container for the bavarian. Press the pulp in a sieve. Reserve 1 cup of juice for the recipe and keep the rest for breakfast. Refrigerate orange cups and caps until needed.

Scratch the skin of the remaining orange and rub the sugar lumps firmly over its surface until they are impregnated with orange essence. Cut the zest (the outer orange coloring), from the orange. Add zest to the milk, bring to a boil, then set aside to infuse for 20 minutes.

Place 1 cup of reserved orange juice and the lemon juice in a saucepan, and reduce to ⅓ cup. Set aside.

Beat sugar and egg yolks together until thick and creamy. Slowly stir the warm milk into the eggs, then add the softened gelatine. Place the custard on medium-low heat and stir continuously until the mixture thickens. Do not allow to approach the boil. Strain through a fine sieve. Add reduced fruit juices and Grand Marnier and leave to cool in the refrigerator, stirring occasionally.

When the mixture is just beginning to set, whip the cream until thickened but not stiff. Stir into the custard. Cover and refrigerate until set.

Press the raspberries through a sieve to remove their seeds. Sweeten the purée just slightly to taste. Put to chill.

Place the almonds in boiling water and parboil for 4 minutes. Slip off the skins and wrap the nuts in plastic wrap.

To assemble the dessert, heap the oranges with scoops of Bavarian and place the caps on top. (Cut a small slice from the bottom to allow the oranges to sit upright if necessary.) Place an orange on a dinner plate. Surround it with raspberry sauce which should float to the rim. Circle 8 softened almonds in the sauce around each orange. (There will be some additional Bavarian left over.)   Serves 10

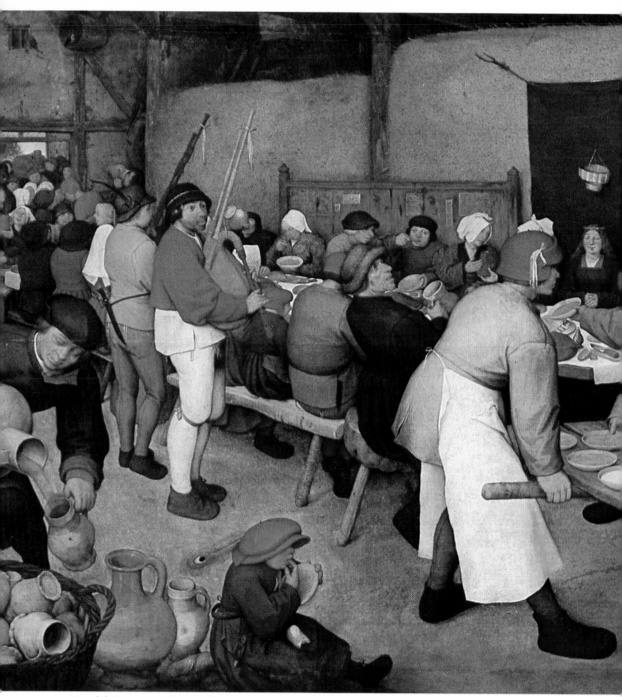

P. Brueghel, *The Peasant Wedding*. Saskia/Editorial Photocolor Archives

A BRUEGHEL PEASANT CELEBRATION

The Inspiration

. . . the colorful painting The Peasant Wedding, *by the sixteenth-century Flemish artist Pieter Brueghel the Elder.*

Brueghel was a master at capturing on canvas the exuberant spontaneity of festivals and carnivals, of dances and weddings; in so doing, he recorded again and again those foodstuffs of his time with which people celebrated. In carnival scenes, pancakes and puddings are baking in the streets; sausages are sizzling; crisp waffles, flavored with cloves and saffron, are dripping with butter in the hands of small children about to devour them. In one painting called *The Land of Cockaigne*, Brueghel created a fantasy of food. The roof of a house is tiled with cakes and pies and surrounded by a fence of link sausages. In the distance, great mountains of porridge stand mounded against the sky, while a small weevil (which on closer inspection turns out to be a man), bores his way through. A boiled pig with a great slice of ham notched from his haunches and a coddled egg on little frog's legs wander by. Under a table laden

A BRUEGHEL PEASANT CELEBRATION

with bread and chicken feet lie three peasants in a drunken stupor. With this peculiar vision, Brueghel intended to show the results of Gluttony, a sin much in the minds of sixteenth-century men, for the age was one of frequent famine and great want. When food was available, people tended to make up in excess for their times of deprivation.

In *The Peasant Wedding* where, one must admit, everyone looks remarkably well fed, the feast is about to begin in an old barn outfitted for the occasion. Behind the lumpen bride hangs a coarse cloth and a bridal headdress to mark her as the honored guest. On the wall are two sheaves of garnered wheat, both luck and fertility for the married couple. A serving man pours small beer into a pitcher, while another two waiters carry an old door as a makeshift serving tray from which one of the guests helpfully passes along the bowls of mush and clotted cream. A dog waits expectantly under the table; a small boy intently licks his dish and fingers. There is a spirit so simple, so convivial, so appealingly informal, that one can hardly view the painting without wishing to step over the frame and into the vivid tableau.

Setting the Scene

Brueghel's expectant scene gives rise to one of the most pleasant Entertainments I can think of. The occasion is amusing and the camaraderie that ensues when everyone must eat communally and with their fingers ensures that even the most rigid or self-conscious of guests will soon relax. It is impossible to gnaw bones and retain dignities.

In a dining room or kitchen, arrange a long table that can accommodate all guests. Run a length of white sheeting or natural canvas or burlap down its center. (If the feast is held outdoors, a long picnic table with benches or doors on top of trestles and bales of straw to sit on would be effective.)

Near the head of the table, hang from a rope a large backdrop of forest green or maize-colored burlap. The only other decoration will be two "sheaves" of wheaten bread (meant to be consumed), which can either be crossed and propped on the table, or fastened against the burlap. Tie around the neck of each guest an ample, covering napkin. (Consider Brueghel's use of strong, unpatterned colors: reds, greens, azure blues, golden browns.) At every place setting there should be a large platter and a mug or tankard for cider, beer, or hearty red wine. Silverware should be kept to a minimum: forks for mashing potatoes; a few rustic knives with bone or wooden handles that can be shared for spearing meat and potatoes. There should also be two or three bowls in which bones and woody asparagus ends can be discarded, and a crock or two of butter.

Serve the first-course soup and encourage everyone to sup directly from the bowls. Remove soup dishes, and place platters of asparagus, ribs, and potatoes and bowls of dipping sauces down the table's center. After this course is cleared, it will be necessary to brush away crumbs and to offer toothpicks and fingerbowls of warm, sweetly perfumed water in which people can cleanse their hands.

Place spiced cakes and bowls of whipped cream on table. Again, guests must break off their own portions and dip them in cream.

Somewhere in the dining area, a yellow light bulb or an amber lighting gel should be inserted so that an antique glow can suffuse the scene. Jigs and reels or southern mountain music (without vocals) make a pleasant accompaniment to the feast.

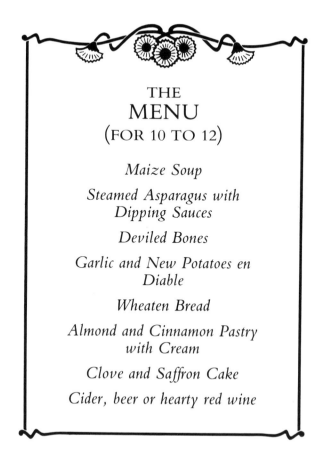

THE
MENU
(FOR 10 TO 12)

Maize Soup

*Steamed Asparagus with
Dipping Sauces*

Deviled Bones

*Garlic and New Potatoes en
Diable*

Wheaten Bread

*Almond and Cinnamon Pastry
with Cream*

Clove and Saffron Cake

Cider, beer or hearty red wine

Maize Soup

3 ounces lean salt pork
4 tablespoons unsalted butter
2 large onions, sliced fine
6 medium-large, all-purpose potatoes, peeled and diced
6 cups cooked, whole-kernel yellow corn, fresh or frozen (do
    not use canned)
3 cups milk, scalded
2 teaspoons salt
Freshly ground pepper
1 *bouquet garni* (celery, parsley, thyme, bay leaf, a leaf of sage)
2 cups heavy cream, warmed
3 egg yolks
Paprika
Lumps of butter

FRY THE SALT PORK in a large sauté pan until golden. Strain out the
pork morsels and add butter to the fat in the pan. In the fat, cook the
onions, covered and over low heat, until they are soft and pale gold in
color.

Cook the potatoes in salted boiling water until tender. Drain well.

Combine onions, potatoes, and corn, and purée briefly in a blender
or food processor (the consistency should be that of a rough gruel). Place
the purée in a pan and add hot milk, salt, pepper, and *bouquet garni*. Heat
to just short of a boil, stirring all the time, then set aside for at least 2
hours.

Just before serving, remove the *bouquet garni* and gently warm the
soup. Beat the cream into the egg yolks, stir some hot soup into the
cream, then slowly add the cream mixture to the soup. Heat and stir
until piping hot, but do not allow to boil. Taste for seasoning.

Ladle the soup into bowls or soup plates and sprinkle each portion
lightly with paprika.
Serves 10

STEAMED ASPARAGUS WITH DIPPING SAUCES

	6 to 8 large stalks asparagus per person 2 whole canned pimientos
Vinaigrette:	1 teaspoon salt Freshly ground pepper 1 tablespoon Dijon-style mustard ⅓ cup red wine vinegar 1 generous cup olive oil 3 tablespoons finely minced parsley
Butter:	2 sticks unsalted butter Salt 1 clove garlic, minced
Sauce Mousseline:	1 stick plus 3 tablespoons unsalted butter 4 egg yolks (from large eggs) 4 tablespoons cold water ½ teaspoon salt Freshly ground pepper, preferably white 3 tablespoons lemon juice ½ cup heavy cream

FOR THE VINAIGRETTE, combine salt, pepper, mustard, and vinegar and let sit until the salt has melted. Beat in the olive oil with a fork and taste carefully for seasoning. Add more vinegar if you prefer. Stir in the parsley. Serve cold.

For the melted butter, place butter, a light sprinkling of salt, and garlic in a pan and melt over low heat. Remove the foam from the top of the butter with a spoon. Let the butter sit for 15 minutes, then strain. Serve warm.

For the Sauce Mousseline, melt butter and keep it very hot. Put egg yolks and cold water in a small, heavy-bottomed pan. Place the pan over brisk heat and whisk continuously as the yolks thicken. Lift the pan on and off the heat as necessary to keep the eggs from hardening, but whisk steadily until the mixture is very thick. Off the heat, pour in a tablespoon of hot butter, whisk until blended, then continue adding butter by small tablespoon additions until half of it is used. Pour in the remaining butter in an even stream and whisk over low heat until very thick. (Again, do not allow to over-heat.) Add salt, pepper, and lemon juice.

Quickly whip the cream until stiff and stir into the sauce. This sauce can be held over warm water until needed, but it cannot be served overly hot or it will separate.

Trim any small unsightly portions of woody stems from the asparagus but, for the most part, leave them whole. Tie the asparagus into 3 or 4 bundles and cook them in a steamer, or steam them standing upright in a large, covered pot with 2 or 3 inches of water.

Lift out the bunches, cut the strings, and arrange the asparagus on 2 platters. Fan the asparagus into sheaves to continue the Entertainment's wheaten motif. Cut the pimiento into wide strips and place them to look like binding cord about the bunches.

Note: The asparagus can be served hot or lukewarm. Divide each sauce into 2 portions and place clusters of sauce dishes at either end of the table. Or guests may be given helpings of each sauce in ceramic snail pots. *Serves at least 12 people*

DEVILED BONES

5 sections of beef plate ribs, 8 bones per section
    (3 to 4 bones per serving)
Salt
Cayenne
Olive oil
1 stick butter
⅔ cup white wine vinegar
2 cups red wine
1 very large onion, minced
2 tablespoons brown sugar
3 cloves garlic, minced or pressed
4 tablespoons Dijon-style mustard
¼ cup soy sauce
14 ounces catsup

TRIM THE PLATE SECTIONS of any overly large portions of fat, particularly on the back indented side of the bones, and wipe them dry. Season generously with salt and cayenne, and sprinkle the plates lightly with olive oil. Rub the oil and seasoning evenly into the beef and place the plates in a large baking pan or dutch oven.

Place all remaining ingredients except the catsup in a saucepan and bring to a boil. Cook for 2 minutes. Pour the hot marinade over the beef

and leave at room temperature for 2 hours. Turn the plates frequently so that all sides receive the benefit of the marinade.

Preheat the oven to 300 degrees.

Lift the sections from the marinade and place each on a large sheet of heavy-duty aluminum foil. Pour the marinade into a saucepan and cook, reducing over medium heat for 15 minutes. Stir in the catsup.

Brush two-thirds of the marinade over the beef plates and wrap up each section in its foil. Bake in roasting pans for 1½ hours.

Open the foil and divide the remaining marinade over the beef. Close up the foil and bake for another hour. Remove the foil and let the plates brown and crisp for another 30 minutes (baste once during this period). The meat can now be held, covered, in a warm oven for 30 minutes or so with no harm done.

Slice the plates into rib sections (this can be rustically executed at table if you wish), heap them up on platters, and serve.   Serves 10 to 12

GARLIC AND NEW POTATOES EN DIABLE

The *diable* is a handsome French unglazed clay pot that functions as a dry roasting unit for potatoes or chestnuts. When it is purchased, the *diable* is first rinsed and cleaned and then never washed again. Like a well-garlicked salad bowl, the dish itself adds to the flavor of the ingredients placed in it and, in the case of the *diable*, the earthy flavor of the clay impregnates and compliments its roasting contents. True *diables* are sometimes available at specialty cookware shops, but another unglazed clay cooker with a cover can be substituted easily. Or one might use 2 or 3 clean 8-inch flowerpots. Stop the bottom holes with a wadded plug of foil, and tie 2 layers of heavy foil over the tops of the pots to act as covers.

5 to 6 pounds new potatoes (3 to 4 per person)
5 to 6 large heads garlic (5 to 6 cloves per person)
Bay leaves
Sprigs of thyme or dried leaf thyme
Butter
Salt and pepper

WASH AND LIGHTLY SCRUB THE POTATOES as needed and dry them well.

Separate heads of garlic into cloves by pressing down on the side of the heads with the flat of the hand until they break apart. Remove excessive skins, but basically leave the cloves encased within their papery coverings.

For each *diable*, combine potatoes, garlic cloves, 2 or 3 bay leaves, and a good sprinkling of thyme. (In the summer, I like to make even a large nesting bed of fresh herbs in the pot.) Place the pot in the oven and turn the heat on to 250 degrees. After 10 minutes, turn the heat up to 350 degrees. Bake for 45 minutes to an hour, depending on whether you admire a slight firmness in potatoes.

Uncover the pot at table so everyone can enjoy the delicious aroma that wafts from the dish. The potatoes should be eaten as follows: Each guest prepares his or her own portion by pressing down first on the garlic cloves until the soft pulp slips from the skins. Then the guest mashes the potatoes, garlic pulp, and a lump of butter together, seasons the mess with salt and pepper, and eats it.

Note: Another equally good variation on this theme is to place all ingredients in a large roasting pan and to coat them lightly with olive oil. Cover and bake until tender. Serve with a pitcher of olive oil to use in the mashing instead of butter.

WHEATEN BREADS

3 recipes Fresh Bread dough (see page 142)
1 egg yolk mixed with 1 tablespoon water

MAKE THE BREAD, divide it into 2 separate batches, and leave to rise until doubled in bulk.

Preheat oven to 350 degrees.

Working with the first batch made, gently punch down the dough and set aside one-third of it. Roll the dough back and forth under the palms of your hands until a long sausage shape forms. Roll out the dough with a rolling pin to gain width. (The length should be as long as possible. Consider both the length of your longest baking sheet and your oven. Two flat cookie sheets can be overlapped so that it is possible to make a "sheaf" that will be a good 20 to 22 inches long.) Place the dough on a lightly oiled pan and curve the top. Pinch in the dough about ¼ of the way from the top. With a knife, cut long strips to resemble stems and, above the pinched section, cut short, fat portions of dough for the heads of wheat. Fan them out slightly. Use the remaining portion of dough to add shorter stems and more heads of wheat on top of the rolled dough for a dimensional effect. (Attach the additions with a slight moistening of water.) Bind the sheaf at its indentation under the heads with 3 or 4 lengths of dough "rope." Use scissors to quickly snip the heads of wheat into individual grains. If you are a slow worker and the day is warm and the dough is rising responsively, place it in the oven immediately. Let the bread rise an additional few minutes if the day is cold. The loaf should look risen and appear plump before it is put to bake.

Compose the second sheaf. Each bread should bake for around 40 minutes or until nicely golden. Protect any over-browning portions with aluminum foil. Remove loaves and let them cool on the baking sheets so that escaping steam can soften the undercrusts somewhat.

Place on table and let each guest break off individual portions.

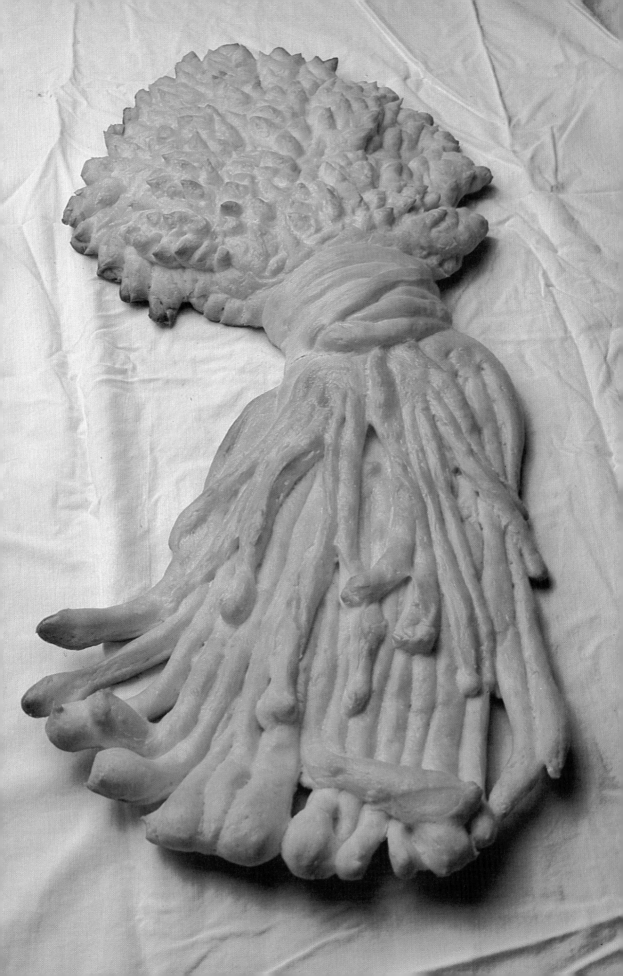

CLOVE AND SAFFRON CAKE

1 teaspoon dry yeast
2 tablespoons warm water
¼ teaspoon powdered saffron
6 good scrapings of nutmeg
1 stick unsalted butter, at room temperature
1 large egg
2 tablespoons white wine (either sweet or dry is interesting)
2 tablespoons honey
1½ cups all-purpose flour, sifted
Pinch of salt
⅔ cup confectioners sugar

An unpainted metal coat hanger

ADD YEAST TO THE WATER and stir in saffron and nutmeg. Let sit until the yeast has dissolved.

In a bowl, beat and stir the butter with a heavy spoon. Add egg, wine, honey, and yeast, and stir until blended (the mixture will not be smooth).

Sieve the flour and salt over the liquid ingredients and mix the dough with your hand until it is soft and smooth. Knead slowly for 5 minutes, then put the dough in a lightly greased bowl, cover it with a towel, and leave to rise for 2 hours.

Lightly butter and flour a 12-inch pizza pan. Place the dough in the pan and press it down and out with your fingertips. Use a lightly floured tumbler to roll the dough out to the edge of the pan as evenly as possible. Press the tongs of a fork around the edge to make a decorative border. Let rise 20 minutes.

Preheat the oven to 375 degrees.

Sieve the confectioners sugar over the top of the cake. Place the pastry in the oven for 12 to 15 minutes or until lightly browned at the edges. Let the cake cool briefly, then slip it onto a basket or serving platter.

Holding the coat hanger by one side with a pot holder, heat its long wire by resting it directly on or in a fire. When it is very hot, use it to imprint a waffled design on the cake. Make 2 or 3 lines, then wipe the hanger with paper towels and reheat it until hot enough to continue the pattern.

Serves 8

ALMOND AND CINNAMON PASTRY WITH CREAM

9 sheets strudel or filo dough
1 stick unsalted butter, melted
¾ cup coarsely ground whole almonds
Cinnamon
¾ cup sugar
Cognac
Heavy cream, lightly whipped and sweetened or, if you prefer,
    natural yogurt

PREPARE THE DOUGH according to package directions. (If it is frozen, it must thaw overnight in the refrigerator before use.) Cut a large piece of heavy plastic (trash-bag weight) to use as a cover for the opened dough. Assemble all ingredients.

Preheat oven to 350 degrees.

Brush a 12-inch pizza pan with some melted butter. Place on the pan 2 sheets of dough, overlapping them on their long edges so that they form a covering square. Immediately brush the square completely with melted butter. (The unrolled stack of dough should be covered with plastic so that it does not dry while the cake is being assembled.)

Place 2 more sheets over the first 2 and brush again with butter. Sprinkle ¼ cup of nuts over the dough so that they cover an 11-inch circumference on the pan. Shake a good ½ teaspoon of cinnamon over the nuts, then sprinkle on a third of the sugar. Place a thumb over the opening of the cognac bottle and very lightly moisten the sugar. Drizzle a third of the melted butter over the sugar.

Repeat the dough step by placing another 2 sheets over the top of the nuts and brushing them with butter, and then top with 2 more sheets and butter again.

As before, sprinkle on another third of the nuts, cinnamon, sugar, cognac, and butter. Round the square by cutting off the corners with a knife. Fold the extra dough up and over the filling to form a rustic round that should now be entirely on the pan. Brush the top of the pastry with butter.

Cut the remaining sheet of dough into 3 long sections. Brush with butter and roll up each length along the wide edge. Curl the rolls in a continuous spiral on top of the pastry. Combine the remaining sugar and nuts and sprinkle generously with cinnamon. Spread the nuts along the path between the spirals. Drizzle the last butter and cognac over the nuts and place the pastry in the oven for 20 to 25 minutes. Protect from over-browning with foil, if necessary. This pastry can be baked ahead and reheated, but it should be served warm. Break off crumbly portions or cut them with a knife.   Serves 10

Matisse, *Still Life with Oysters*. Editorial Photocolor Archives

A
MATISSE
PATTERNED
LUNCHEON

The Inspiration

. . . the joyful, explosive paintings of food upon the table that flowed from the artist Matisse.

I n canvas after canvas he shaped and textured colors, primary in their intensity, into dazzling displays of pattern against pattern, color against color, and brilliant arabesques. He arranged forms and objects in traditional ways—a lemon, say, beside a dish—then painted the mere suggestion of the fruit with a brush or two of citron yellow as casually applied as if it were with fingerpaints. And yet the fruit is no less a lemon for this apparent indifference. (Indeed, it even intensifies in "lemonness" if that is possible.)

He painted an entire table a single hue of red and placed upon it a clear glass wine decanter. Then, in total disregard for the true perspective of the scene, he painted white behind the bottle, as if it floated there in watery space and its own

A Matisse
Patterned
Luncheon

contradictory aura. He frequently set a
swatch of black behind a vivid object, like
a black plate beneath a butter lump,
instead of shadow. He set undulating
patterns over and against each other in
complex yet ordered designs that vibrate
before the eyes.

The result is pure seduction, pure
sensuosity, and a glowing dynamic that
translates effectively to the dinner table.
And if Matisse's artistic style is not hard to
reproduce, the subject matter is even
easier. Over and over Matisse painted
eggplants, green apples, and lemons;
oranges, limes, and pears. And the colors
would be so perfect that one impeccable
dab of rusted purple could represent an
eggplant. He painted oyster shells with
outlines of fat, squiggly black, and
pineapples for the tapestry of their skin.
He adored split-leaf philodendrons and the
reds and lavenders of anemones, which he
stuck as if by fistfuls into flat,
undimensional vases. No possible color
combination ever frightened him or gave
him pause, from the energy of salmon and
vermilion set next to blue and green, to
the flame of yellow, emerald, and ruby
pulsating against violet and electric cobalt
blue.

Setting the Scene

Turn to books on Matisse for a multitude of ideas, then set a table with opposing patterns of powerful form and colorful contrast. Choose a diagonal grid of stripes for the background cloth, then a rounded, repetitive design for a placemat to be set directly over the cloth. Yet a third material, of strong color but diminutive pattern, can be used for a napkin. Use if possible rectangular tables and placemats, for Matisse liked the converging planes of straight angles in his paintings. Arrange each place setting as if it were a painting, and place the mats at a variety of angles under each dinner plate.

Consider the drama of clearing the entire table after the main course, then placing a new cloth, with a billowing flourish, over the old. Replace the mats with others of bold color beneath the dessert.

Select several patterns directly from the paintings then reproduce them in a display of small canapés and sandwiches.

Use patterns from Matisse's series of gouache paper cut-out designs. Form breads into those shapes, and place them at random about the table.

Sacrifice a split-leaf philodendron plant and use its leaves and a pineapple for the centerpiece.

For background music, choose the single, clear voice of a solo instrument—the piano works of Satie, perhaps.

THE
MENU
(FOR 6)

Patterned Canapés

Cut-out Breads

Clams and Oysters on a Bed of Salt

Chicken and Vegetables en Gelée

Iced Fruits

*Wine: Pinot Chardonay or
Macon*

Patterned Canapés

	3 to 4 2-inch squares of crustless bread, per person (white, light or dark rye, or a variety)
Choose from a variety of colorful ingredients and spreads:	Black olives, caviar Red pimiento, red caviar Salmon smoked salmon slices, Paprika Butter Pink sliced ham Yellow crumbled hard-boiled egg yolk, Mustard Butter Green olives, capers, watercress petals, Herb Butter Brown anchovy filets White hard-boiled egg white, Cream Cheese with Garlic

TO MAKE PAPRIKA BUTTER: Cream 1 stick unsalted butter with 1 teaspoon paprika, a few grains of cayenne, and just enough tomato paste to produce the desired shade of salmon.

TO MAKE MUSTARD BUTTER: Cream 1 stick unsalted butter with 3 tablespoons of Dijon-style mustard. Grind in some white pepper, and add the sieved yolks of 2 hard-boiled eggs.

TO MAKE HERB BUTTER: Briefly parboil 2 well-packed cups of greens (mixed spinach, parsley, chives, a bit of tarragon, if possible) in salted water. When they are wilted but still vivid, drain and refresh under cold water. Squeeze very dry and purée, along with 1 stick of unsalted butter, in a food processor or blender. Add salt, pepper, and small gratings of fine lemon zest to taste.

TO MAKE CREAM CHEESE WITH GARLIC: Soften 6 ounces of cream cheese and add a few drops of cream to bring it to spreading consistency. Using a garlic press, add garlic to taste. Add freshly ground white pepper and a bit of salt.

To assemble canapés, lightly toast the bread if desired. The display will be most effective if 2 or 3 basic patterns are used. Arrange the bread into a large rectangle on a serving board. Decide on the basic pattern. Spread ham, salmon, or colored butters onto the bread squares to lay down the basic color. (Use a wide pastry brush to spread butters, and allow the brush strokes to show.) Alternating diagonal strips can be made by piping on butters with a plain pastry tube or cutting strips of pimiento, ham, or anchovy filets. Caviar and egg yolk might be carefully spooned into a pattern. Make use of patterned cookie cutters and cut some small designs which can be decorated, then superimposed on other canapés. Repetitive designs, like the little cat's paw markings that Matisse liked, can be made from olives or capers and placed against light backgrounds. Compose the canapés as close to consumption as possible, and cover them lightly with plastic wrap to keep the butters and meats from discoloring.

CUT-OUT BREADS

    1 recipe Fresh Bread dough (page 142)
    1 egg yolk beaten with 2 teaspoons water for glaze

USE MATISSE'S CUT-OUT GOUACHE DESIGNS of dancing shapes, rosettes, and palm or philodendron leaves as inspiration. Make the bread dough and let it rise once. Punch down and form the shapes directly on an oiled baking pan. Let the projections be half as narrow as the design suggests to allow for rising. These breads will be slightly too large to serve as individual portions; 1 bread should be formed to serve 2 people. Brush the tops of the breads with egg yolk glaze and leave to rise for 15 minutes before baking. Preheat oven to 375 degrees.

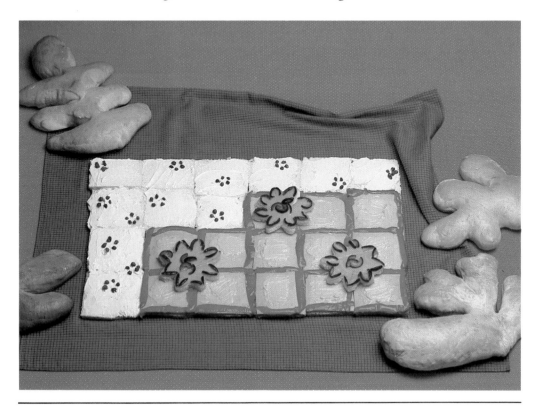

Just before baking, do any cosmetic tucking and reforming necessary, and do not hesitate to gently pinch in knobs or rounds of dough that have over-expanded.

Bake for around 30 to 35 minutes, or until the breads are nicely browned. Makes 6 to 8 breads

CLAMS AND OYSTERS ON A BED OF SALT

Rock salt
6 to 8 clams, oysters, or a mixture of both, per person
Finely minced parsley and chives
Finely minced green pepper
Finely minced ham
Salt
Cayenne
Paprika
Dry white wine
Lemons and lemon juice
Parsley sprigs

1-inch squares of aluminum foil

PREHEAT THE OVEN TO 300 DEGREES. If you have heatproof dishes for each person, arrange beds of rock salt on them. If not, layer the salt into a baking pan and have individual dishes, with generous salt on them, ready to receive the shellfish. Place ovenproof dishes or roasting pan in warm oven for 15 minutes. Preheat a broiler and regulate the flame to medium.

Have the shellfish open, with the clams or oysters on the half shell. Sprinkle each with a pinch of minced parsley and chives and a pinch each of green pepper and ham. Season lightly with salt and a few grains of cayenne and paprika.

Arrange the shellfish on the warm salt, add a few drops of wine to each shell, and cover the clams or oysters with squares of foil.

Broil for around 5 minutes, then remove the foil and continue cooking for another 5 minutes.

Have each place setting prepared with lemons and parsley edging, an informally placed napkin, and a small carafe of wine. (Place a white saucer beneath it to imitate Matisse's perverse perspectives.) Place the plates on the table, on trivets if necessary, and be sure to arrange 1 clam or oyster off the plate and to the right side.

CHICKEN AND VEGETABLES EN GELÉE

The following ingredients are for a 13-inch-long oval quiche pan, or an 11-inch rectangular gratin dish. Make this dish a day ahead.

6 breasts of chicken, boned
6 cups well-seasoned chicken stock, preferably homemade
5 carrots, scraped and trimmed
5 stalks celery, strung and trimmed
1½ pounds asparagus *or* tender green beans
Scallions
1 egg white and 1 egg shell
1 envelope gelatine
¼ cup cold water
3 or 4 parsley stalks
1 cup fresh or frozen green peas, cooked
A few slivers of black olives

Herb or mustard-flavored mayonnaise

POACH THE CHICKEN BREASTS in the stock for 30 minutes over very low heat. Lift out the breasts and remove the skin. Trim and use only the wing-shaped suprême portion for this dish. Cover and refrigerate the chicken.

Strain the stock and discard the last few sullied spoonfuls. Refrigerate until chilled, then lift off all surface fat.

Prepare the vegetables. Some will be sliced and used to cover the bottom of the dish. Others will be cut into strips to garnish a surface pattern on top. Make ⅔ cup each of carrots and celery, cut into uniform strips 2 inches long and ½ inch wide. Cut the same amount of asparagus tips or green beans into 2-inch lengths. Parboil these vegetables in salted water until just tender but still slightly crisp and brightly colored. Strain out, refresh under cold water, and chill.

Slice remaining carrots, celery, asparagus or beans, and whites of scallions (reserve tops) into thin rounds. Add to the same water and again parboil until tender-crisp. Drain and refresh under cold water. Refrigerate.

To assemble the dish, wipe the breasts dry and place them down the length of the dish, overlapping them slightly so that a clear border remains around the edge. Spread the sliced vegetable rounds around the edge.

Whisk the egg white and crumbled shell together until light and frothy. Soften the gelatine in cold water. Combine egg white and shell, gelatine, stock, parsley stalks, and 1 or 2 chopped scallion tops in a heavy saucepan. Heat gently and whisk continuously until the mixture comes to a boil. A thick matting of albumen and vegetable stalks will form, and all impurities will attach to it. As soon as the boil is reached, stop stirring and let the stock maintain a low boil for 15 minutes. Cover, remove from heat, and let sit, undisturbed, for 10 minutes.

Rinse a clean dish towel with cold water, wring it out, then use it to line a large sieve. Place the sieve over a deep bowl and, carefully and slowly, pour in the hot broth. Let it drip through of its own accord, and do not allow the bottom of the sieve to touch the clear liquid beneath.

Pour some of the glistening stock over the chicken and vegetables, adding just enough so that the vegetables are covered. Place dish in refrigerator and chill until firm. Arrange a border of orange carrot, green bean, and white celery strips around the edge of the chicken. Space green peas around the edge. Place a few olive slivers in a contrasting pattern against the white chicken. Pour over the remaining stock and refrigerate dish until needed.

Serve with an herb or mustard-flavored mayonnaise.   Serves 6

ICED FRUITS

1 large grapefruit, with a pretty skin
4 large navel oranges
1 pint lime sherbet
Juice of 1 lime
1 pint lemon sherbet
Juice of 1 lemon
1 cup sieved raspberry purée, from frozen or fresh berries

USING A MELON BALLER, cut a round plug from the stem ends of the grapefruit and oranges. Over a large bowl, dig into the fruits and scrape out all pulp. Use a finger if necessary to detach pith, and clean the fruits until they are perfectly smooth on the interior. Place shells in the freezer.

Press the pulp through a sieve and reserve the juice.

Place lime sherbet, lime juice, and ½ cup of the citrus juice in a food processor or blender, and blend until smooth and loose. Scoop the green ice into 2 of the hollowed oranges (using an iced tea spoon is the easiest method). Replace in freezer.

Divide the lemon sherbet into 2 bowls. To one add the juice of the lemon and ½ cup of citrus juice. Soften the mixture. Fill the other 2 orange shells and place in freezer.

To the remaining lemon sherbet, add the raspberry purée. Stir until soft, then fill the grapefruit. Freeze.

Let solidify in the freezer overnight. To serve, slice the fruits in half by cutting down through the small filling hole (rather than slicing them through the middle). Two orange halves or 1 grapefruit half make up a serving.

Serves 6

Note: For display purposes, simply place the cut halves around the pineapple centerpiece, and let each guest choose an iced fruit.

Monet, *Water Lilies I*. Courtesy, Museum of Fine Arts, Boston. Gift of Edward Jackson Holmes

A MONET WATER LILY LUNCHEON

The Inspiration

. . . Monet's remarkable eye for light and shadow, and his extraordinary series of water lily paintings.

For this late spring luncheon, what could be more refreshing than to eat floating on the surface of a brilliant, cooling, flower-bedecked lily pond? If there is no better artist than Matisse to teach us brilliance, pattern, and color, there is also no better artist than Monet from whom to study radiance and luminosity. It is most natural to turn to Monet for inspiration, for the master impressionist loved to eat and drink and did so with a Frenchman's obsessive passion. Luncheon parties, his cook tells us in a memoir, were splendid affairs, with expensive wines and the freshest, most impeccable ingredients simply prepared. Look sometime at one of the albums about Monet's life at Giverny, his beautiful pink home in the Normandy countryside. There are a wealth of faded photographs

A MONET
WATER LILY
LUNCHEON

celebrating the innumerable festivities, and in each of them the artist stands, patriarchally bearded, dressed in a floppy Panama hat, a jacket snugly buttoned over his ample *embonpoint*. In the pictures are the guests: ladies in floating summer dresses, children solemn under bonnets, and the likes of Whistler, Clemenceau, Rodin. First, the guests would congregate in the glassed studio to view the latest paintings. Then, past the fowling pen and the large turkeys which Monet once painted (a brilliant rendering of white birds in shadow, with wattles like bright rubies and one ravishing spot of light blazing through the feathers of the cock), they would pass into the endless gardens with their dazzling display of blooms, great swatches of floral color as if some artist-gardener had sewn whole packages of seeds. And then to the amazing lily pond that Monet himself established by diverting water from the nearby Epte River.

Here the photographs were taken, the paintings painted. A Japanese footbridge spans the narrowed waist of the pond; willows weep into the water; yellow, pink, and white lilies open in the mid-morning sun. Monet, accompanied by his stepdaughter Blanche, would set his easel near the water's edge and paint furiously. Canvas after canvas would be started, only to be set aside after a few minutes. No, he would say, I can work on this no longer, the light is completely different. And it was that elusive light that his eye and brush sought to capture . . . the moment's transient luminosity. The paintings show it all. Up close, the stab of blue-white paint captures a mote of light upon the pond, the streaks of color blur before the eyes, but stand back from those mammoth paintings and there is all the light and beauty of a summer's day reflected in the cooling, blissful waters.

Setting the Scene

Imagine then a table as Monet might have designed it, all flow and eddies, swirls, reflections, glittering light and lustrous pastels with food to match. First take a round table and cover it with mauve or lavender, a dusty pink or patterned water blue. A moiré satin, a polished cotton, the faintest paisley print—any of these would do. Cover the cloth with glass cut to the size of the table, or use individual placemats of mirror or glass, always round. (Monet delighted in the circular form of lilies and their leaves, and he instructed his gardeners to cut back the prolific plants so that each remaining clump of flowers, when viewed from a distance, appeared in form like an oversized lily leaf floating on the surface.)

In the middle of the table, in a large glass bowl half-filled with water, are one or two white flowers—magnolias or chrysanthemums or water lilies—and large green floating leaves. The plates are green or white, the silver is polished to a fine sheen. At least two wine glasses, one a large ballon (Burgundy), are at each place setting. Starched white napkins folded into lotus shape are to the left of each setting, some higher, some lower as if placed at random. Swimming by each guest's plate is a plump roll in the shape of a fish. All other implements on the table should be highly reflective: silver or glass salt shakers, cut-crystal bowls for dressings, glass dessert dishes.

Ideally this meal will be out of doors, with the table set against a backdrop of greenery. If it is in the dining room, fill the room with plants. To add luminous reflections to the table, try a photographer's trick. Place a sheet of gold or silver foil so that a light source can bounce off it and down onto the tabletop. Or make use of prisms and their ability to cast rainbows. On the phonograph, Handel's *Water Music* or Debussey's *La Mer* would provide a gentle accompaniment.

When the salad is served, place the garnishing chopped herbs and lavender flowers in a small bowl. Instead of presenting the salads already garnished, serve them plain; then, when all the plates are on the table, like a bridal attendant scattering rose petals, flourish on the flowers and herbs with a pretty gesture, like small painted strokes across the table, around the centerpiece, over the salads, everywhere.

THE
MENU
(FOR 8)

*Spring Onion Soup with
Watercress Purée*

*Scallop and Spinach Terrine
with Herbed Mayonnaise*

*Artichoke and Green Bean
Salad with Walnut
Dressing and
Goat Cheese*

Sesame Bread Fish

*Molded Lemon Pudding with
Sabayon*

Wine: Chardonnay or Aligoté

Spring Onion Soup with Watercress Purée

2 bunches watercress
4 cups thinly sliced spring onions (white and
    tender green portions)
4 tablespoons unsalted butter
3 rounded tablespoons flour
2 cups chicken stock
2 cups milk
4 egg yolks
1 cup heavy cream
Salt and pepper

Garnish: Thinly sliced rounds of spring onion greens

HAVE A SMALL POT OF WATER AT THE BOIL. Prepare the watercress by selecting good leaves and tender stems. Plunge the leaves into the water and blanch for 30 seconds. Drain and refresh under cold water. Gather the watercress into a towel, and twist until the mass of green is as dry as possible. Set aside.

Place onions, butter, and ½ cup of water in a heavy saucepan. Cover and let the onions cook over very low heat until they are purée tender. Stir frequently, for on no account should they brown and caramelize. When the onions are tender, sprinkle the flour over them and stir over low heat for 2 minutes.

Combine chicken stock and milk in a saucepan and bring to a boil. Off the heat, whisk the liquid slowly into the onions. Return soup to heat and simmer for 20 minutes.

Beat the egg yolks with ⅔ cup of cream in a bowl. Slowly whisk in a ladle of hot soup, then add the remainder of the soup in a steady stream. Return soup to its pan and cook, stirring constantly, until it thickens somewhat. Do not allow to boil. Strain soup through a fine sieve and taste for seasoning. A bit more milk may be added if soup seems too thick. Keep warm.

Place the watercress and ⅓ cup of cream in a food processor. Process just until the cream thickens and becomes a uniform green.

To serve the soup, ladle portions into individual soup bowls and place a dollop of watercress cream in the center of each serving. Use the tip of a spoon to swirl the green cream lightly against the white soup. Sprinkle with sliced onion greens.

Serves 8

SCALLOP AND SPINACH TERRINE
WITH HERBED MAYONNAISE

The following scallop dish can be made in a traditional terrine or, more imaginatively, it can be baked in a round mold by using a 3-pound (48-ounce) shortening can. Remove the outer paper from the can, butter the interior, and layer in the scallop mixture. Bake with the can standing upright in water. After weighting and chilling, simply use a can opener to remove the bottom, then press out the terrine and slice into rounds.

1 small onion, chopped fine
1 tablespoon butter
4 ounces fresh mushrooms, cleaned and chopped
    fine
Salt, pepper, nutmeg
10 ounces fresh spinach, washed
1 cup fish stock or clam broth
4 slices firm white bread, crusts removed
1 pound fresh sea scallops plus 6 large scallops,
    rinsed and dried
2 large eggs plus 1 egg white
Mayonnaise, preferably homemade
Lemon juice
1 teaspoon minced fresh herbs (parsley, chives, a
    touch of tarragon, or just parsley)

Garnish: Lemon wedges
    Romaine lettuce cut into chiffonade

COOK THE ONION in butter until soft. Add the mushrooms, increase the heat, and stir while the mushrooms render their liquid. When the bottom of the pan looks completely dry, remove from the heat, season with salt and pepper, and set aside to cool.

Have a pot of simmering water on the stove. Select the 12 largest spinach leaves and carefully pull back and tear off their stems. Briefly dip the leaves into the water, then immediately remove them and spread the leaves on towels.

Stem the remaining spinach and plunge it into the water for 3 minutes. Drain and refresh under cold water. Gather the spinach into a ball and squeeze out as much water as possible. Set aside.

Place the fish stock in a saucepan. Crumble in the bread and bring to a boil. Stir the mass until it appears to be a uniform paste.

Select the 6 largest scallops and cut them vertically in half. Wrap the portions in the whole spinach leaves and squeeze each scallop well so that the encasing green adheres firmly.

Place remaining scallops, moistened bread, ball of cooked spinach, and eggs in the bowl of a food processor. Blend until smooth. Stir in the mushrooms and season with salt, pepper, and a scraping of nutmeg.

Butter a terrine and spoon in a layer of scallop mixture. Space some of the wrapped green scallops in orderly fashion, then continue to build the terrine, ending with a smooth coating of scallop mixture. Lightly cover the terrine with a piece of buttered aluminum foil. Place the dish in a *bain-marie*, cover, and cook on a burner for about 1 hour (the surface should feel firm to the touch). Do not allow the water to boil. Cool until at room temperature, then place a light weight on the surface and refrigerate overnight.

To serve, cut a slice of terrine and center it on a plate. Surround the slice with a fine shred of dark green lettuce and add a lemon wedge on the side. Add herbs and enough lemon juice to the mayonnaise so that it tastes distinctly tart. Pass the sauce separately at table.   Serves 8 to 10

Green Bean and Artichoke Salad with Goat Cheese

32 English walnut halves
1½ pounds tender green beans
2 tablespoons flour
Juice of 1 lemon
8 artichokes
Bibb or Boston lettuce
Small goat *banons* or slices of Saint-Saviol
    Bucheron

Dressing:
⅓ cup red wine vinegar
Salt and pepper
⅓ cup olive oil
⅓ cup walnut oil, or to taste
Minced herbs (parsley, chives)

Garnish:
Parsley and chives, chopped
Lavender-colored flower blossoms (violets,
    chives, borage, or hyssop blossoms)

PREPARE A WALNUT-OIL VINAIGRETTE. Add salt and pepper to vinegar and stir until the salt dissolves. Stir in the oils and herbs and mix with a fork until well blended. Taste for seasoning.

Bring a small pot of water to the boil. Plunge in the walnut halves and boil for 3 minutes. Drain and peel. (Using the fingernails is the easiest method; this is a tiresome chore, but only a few nuts are needed per person.)

Cook the beans in boiling salted water until just tender and still bright green. Drain and refresh.

Bring a large pot of salted water to the boil. Mix the flour with ¼ cup of water and add the paste and the lemon juice to the pot.

Using a stainless-steel knife, cut off the artichoke stems, snap back the leaves, and cut off 1½ inches of each vegetable's top. Trim the artichokes of dark leaf portions until only the hearts remain, the chokes still intact. Cook the artichokes in the acidulated water until a knife point easily pierces the stem end. Strain from the water and lift off the choke portions. Immediately add artichokes to the vinaigrette, turning them well in the oil; then add beans and marinate at room temperature for at least 1 hour before serving.

To serve, prepare a small bed of lettuce leaves on each plate. Place goat cheese portion in the middle, then swirl green beans concentrically around it. Garnish with artichokes, walnuts, herbs, and lavender flowers, and drizzle any remaining dressing over each portion.   Serves 8

SESAME BREAD FISH

1 package (¼ ounce) dry yeast
2 cups warm water
2 tablespoons unsalted butter, melted
2 teaspoons salt
¼ cup sesame seeds, lightly toasted
5½ to 6 cups unbleached flour
1 egg yolk
1 tablespoon milk

Garnish: Sesame seeds

DISSOLVE THE YEAST IN THE WATER. Add melted butter and salt.

Pulverize the toasted sesame seeds in a blender or grind them by hand in a mortar, and add to the yeast.

Stir in flour until a mass of dough forms that is firm enough to turn out onto a counter. Knead the dough for 10 minutes, adding more flour as necessary until it feels smooth and elastic. Try to keep the dough as soft as possible without it being sticky.

Place the dough in a lightly oiled bowl, cover with a towel, and set aside in a warm place to rise for 1 hour or until doubled in bulk.

Heat oven to 375 degrees.

Punch the dough down and, on a clean surface, roll the dough out to a thickness of 1 inch. Let the dough relax for 10 minutes, then cut out fish shapes. Place the dough-fish on an oiled baking sheet. Twist some to the right and left to vary their positions. Fins and scales can be added or imprinted if so desired.

Beat the egg yolk with the tablespoon of milk and brush the glaze over the dough. Sprinkle with whole sesame seeds. Let the breads rest 20 minutes, then place in the oven to bake for around 25 minutes or until nicely browned. (If the fish seem over-crisp, wrap them in a clean dish towel when they are taken from the oven to soften the crust slightly. There should be a chewy, roll-like quality to the fish.)

Place 1 fish per person at random and directly on the tabletop.

Makes about 10 to 15 fish

Molded Lemon Pudding with Sabayon

4 medium lemons
¼ cup mint liquor (crème de menthe)
5 tablespoons sugar
1 stick unsalted butter, softened
⅓ cup all-purpose flour
1¼ cups milk, scalded
5 eggs plus 2 egg whites, separated and at room temperature

Sabayon:
1 egg plus 2 egg yolks
¼ cup sugar
3 tablespoons lemon juice
2 tablespoons dry white wine
1 cup heavy cream, plus additional cream as needed

Garnish:
3 ounced bittersweet chocolate
Candied violets
Candied or fresh mint leaves

BUTTER AND GENEROUSLY SUGAR AN 8-CUP SOUFFLÉ or charlotte mold and refrigerate until needed. (Individual soufflé dishes could also be used).

Heat the oven to 350 degrees.

Cut long strips of zest from 2 lemons. Place the strips, the mint liquor, and 1 tablespoon of sugar in a small, heavy saucepan. Let the zest cook over low heat until the liquid is almost gone and the zest has crystallized. Remove and let harden. Grate a fine zest from the remaining 2 lemons. Squeeze the juice from all 4 lemons.

In a bowl, mix the softened butter, remaining sugar, and the flour to form a thick paste. Stir the hot milk slowly into the flour. Add the finely grated zest and the lemon juice. Return the mixture to a high heat and stir vigorously until the mixture thickens and leaves the side of the pan.

Off the heat, stir in the egg yolks. Beat the whites to firm (but not dry) peaks, and fold into the pudding base. Pour the batter into the sugared mold. Bake in a *bain-marie* for 1 hour. Let the pudding rest for 5 minutes, then unmold it onto a large, rimmed platter. Serve cool.

Melt the chocolate with ⅓ cup of water over low heat.

For the sabayon, place egg and egg yolks, sugar, lemon juice, and wine in a heavy saucepan or sabayon maker. Whisk over low heat until the mixture is thick but pourable. (Move pan off and on heat as necessary to keep eggs from cooking.) Remove pan from heat and continue beating until the sauce is room temperature. Whip 1 cup cream to the same consistency and fold into the egg mixture. Cover and refrigerate until needed.

To assemble, both chocolate and sabayon should be at the same temperature and consistency. Add cream to the sabayon until it is light and pourable, then ladle over the pudding and let it float out to the rim of the serving platter. Spoon drizzles of chocolate onto the floating sauce and let it swirl and eddy. Garnish with crystallized lemon peel, candied violets, and mint leaves.   Serves 8 to 10

WATER LILY NAPKIN FOLD

Have 1 heavily starched white napkin per person. The napkin can be a minimum of 20 inches square, but a 24- or 26-inch napkin is better.

Lay the napkin flat and fold all corners into the center so they meet in neat points. Crease the folds well at every step. Again fold the corners to meet at the center. Fold one more time (a total of 3 folds), and press the napkin down firmly. Turn the napkin over.

Fold the corners of the turned napkin into the center. Holding all the points firmly down in the center with the fingers of the left hand, gently reach under the napkin and start pulling out the petal points (there should be 12 in all).

If some extra "flowers" are desired for decorative effect, 1 or 2 straight pins can be inserted on the underside to ensure that the napkin remains composed. To stiffen an over-limp napkin, try placing a square of heavy aluminum foil on top of the napkin before the first fold is made.

BUTTER FLOWER

Buy a 1-pound block of unsalted butter or slightly soften 4 sticks and press them into the semblance of a rectangle. Refrigerate until hard. Using a wire-strung cheese slicer, scrape across the length of the butter to make a tightly curled central core. Place the core on a sauce plate, then continue scraping "petals" and attaching them around the base of the core until you have a full flower. (Use remaining butter for cooking.) Freeze the flower until solid, then break it off from the plate and place it in a bowl on a bed of crushed ice. Add a few green leaves under the flower.

Managing a Summer's Crowd

Van Gogh, *Olive Trees*. Minneapolis Institute of Arts

LE GRAND
AÏOLI

The Inspiration

*. . . the largest luncheon party I ever attended,
when an entire Provençal village closed down
its commercial enterprises for the afternoon and
turned out, en masse, for le Grand Aïoli.*

The consumption of *aïoli*, that
powerfully aromatic garlic
mayonnaise that seems to hold
within itself the very soul of Provence, is a
serious affair in the South of France. On
meatless Fridays, the *traiteur* shops display
in their windows take-home containers of
cod and green beans, potatoes and
artichokes, a *petite aïoli* for the family. But
once a season, in the height of summer,
the small towns that cling to the herb-
covered hillsides and hide in the fragrant
valleys of the Var honor *aïoli* in a more
dramatic way. Each village has a patron
saint, and on the saint's day begins a three-
day *fête* in his or her honor that will entail
stringing festival lights about the trees and
lining the main street with games of skill
and merry-go-rounds for children. On the
last day of the *fête*, a *Grand Aïoli*, prepared
usually by the local butcher and eaten on
tables in the local park, ends the
celebration.

Five hundred people were there one
summer when I attended. On the cool
stone benches under the broad plane trees,

LE GRAND AÏOLI

we wait for the food, old and young alike,
family and friends gathered to celebrate
Saint Vincent and the abundance of the
fertile region. Soon trucks and vans arrive
and men help the village's lady butcher,
red faced in the heat, to unload basket
after basket of hot, steamed potatoes,
artichokes, carrots, cauliflowers, beans,
beets, and cases of hard-boiled eggs, bowls
of snails, buckets of cod, mortars heaped
with golden *aïoli*.

The mayor, who places himself in
charge of service, urges us to laden our
plates with fish and vegetables, and small
children circulate throughout the crowd
with baskets of sliced bread. Submerged in
a nearby stream is case upon case of rosé
wine, the only proper drink for the
occasion; and because the day is so hot,
and garlic is such a soporific, all the guests
fill their cups with ice cubes to abate the
heady effects of the wine.

Late into the afternoon we sit and eat
and talk, and then the mayor, attempting
to dignify the occasion with a flowery
speech, thanks the cooks, the truck
drivers, the basket passers, the wine
pourers, the honorable guests—in short,
everyone. Then he toasts everyone and
everyone toasts him and toasts continue
until the dancing starts. Someone has
hooked speakers into the trees, and the
music from them ebbs and flows in the
breeze over the crowd. The mayor
partners the plump butcher; elderly ladies,
surprisingly agile in their black widow's
dresses, dance with grandchildren wet
from wading in the stream. Young lovers

cling together in the shadows and, when daylight passes and the sun slips behind the mountains, we dance on into the night, illuminated only by the light of the moon.

Setting the Scene

Preparing *le Grand Aïoli* is one of the easiest and most expandable ways I know to feed a crowd. As an event, it would make a perfect fund-raising dinner for charity or church, for it lends itself to being produced by the joint efforts of many people. (One person is responsible for the making of *aïoli*; another boils the eggs; a third prepares the green beans; and so on.) The meal can be served hot, cold, or at room temperature.

Basically there is no reason why one could not hold this feast at any time of the year, but it pleases most when held out of doors and under a summer's sun. (Outdoor entertaining automatically relaxes guests, for the vaulting, limitless space easily dissipates tensions and ill feelings that can more easily accumulate when people are surrounded with walls and ceilings. Indoors, where man prevails, human nature dominates; outdoors, where more tolerant nature rules, humans—subdued and diminished to their proper proportions—tend to show themselves to better advantage.)

Planning the feast means only calculating ingredients on a per-person basis. Although the elemental foods are easy to prepare, they can be massed together in striking visual array. Spread a buffet table with small, patterned Provençal cloth, and use rustic baskets and clay pots for serving pieces. Little decoration is needed, for the simple display of neatly arrayed vegetables and perhaps a vase of flowers are all that is necessary.

One should be aware of the physiological effects of copious amounts of garlic on the human system, for the potent herb will surely turn guests drowsy in the sun. A thoughtful host will dissipate this tendency with thoroughly chilled rosé wine watered down with ice cubes and with a head-clearing granité; and he or she will enliven the occasion with music, laughter, and dance.

THE
MENU

Niçoise Olives with Herbs

Filigreed Breads

Hard-Boiled Eggs

Artichokes

Green Beans

Cauliflower

Carrots

Beets

New Potatoes

Shrimp in their Shells

Optional: *Chick Peas*
        Roasted Leg of Lamb
        Salt Cod

Aïoli

Minted Lemon Granité

Wine: Iced Rosé

Niçoise Olives with Herbs

Niçoise Olives
Olive oil
Small sprigs of fresh thyme, oregano, savory
Bay leaves

HAVE ONLY SOME BOWLS OF HERB-SCENTED OLIVES to accompany a pre-dinner glass of rosé. If the olives are packed in brine rather than oil, drain them well and pour on a generous coating of olive oil. Mix many herbs, for visual as well as flavoring effect, into the olives, and let them marinate for 2 days before serving. If only dried herbs are available, use bay leaves and crumbled leaf thyme.

Filigreed Bread

1 recipe Fresh Bread dough (page 142) for every 12 to 15 people
1 egg yolk beaten with 1 tablespoon water

MAKE THE BREAD DOUGH and let it rise once. Oil your largest baking sheet (or overlap 2 flat, smaller sheets on an oven rack for more width.)

With no attempt to officially punch down the dough, remove the bread from its rising bowl, place it on the baking sheet, and, using a rolling pin, roll out the dough into the shape of a large, inverted triangle. Leaving 1½ inches intact both at bottom and top, make a long slit down through the length of the dough and spread the opening apart. Cut 3 slanting slits on each side (see photograph, page 109), and again spread the slits wide open, tucking and forming the sections neatly into place. The bread should have a butterfly appearance and be a good 20 inches across at its top. Brush the loaf with egg yolk and water glaze, and leave to rise for 25 to 30 minutes. Preheat oven to 350 degrees.

Immediately before baking, do any gentle cosmetic tucking necessary to open slits or neaten borders. Bake for around 45 to 50 minutes or until richly golden in color and firm on the bottom. If the bread seems over-crisp, let it cool directly on a counter, covered with a kitchen towel so that escaping steam can soften the crust. Place the whole loaves on table and let guests break off portions as needed.

ARTICHOKES

3 tablespoons flour
3 tablespoons water
Salt
1 artichoke per person
1 lemon, halved

MIX FLOUR WITH WATER, then continue diluting with water until the flour is a watery paste. Place a large, non-aluminum pot of well-salted water on the stove, add the flour and the juice of half the lemon, and bring to a boil.

Start breaking off the tails of the artichokes. With a stainless-steel knife, cut off the upper third of the vegetables and use scissors to trim off remaining sharp points on the ends of leaves. Rub the top of each artichoke with the remaining lemon half and, when 3 or 4 have accumulated, drop them into the pan of water.

Cover the pan but leave the lid ajar. Simmer for around 15 minutes or until a fork easily pierces the tail end of the artichokes. Lift out the vegetables with a strainer and let them drain, upside down, on a platter.

GREEN BEANS

8 to 10 tender green beans per person
Salt

STRING THE BEANS by snapping off both ends and gently pulling away the side filaments. Bring a pot of salted water to a fierce boil and drop in the beans. Cover and bring back to a boil as soon as possible. Test the beans by taking 1 out and eating a portion. When the beans are *al dente* and still a vivid green, strain them into a colander and run cool water over them for 1 minute to set their color.

CAULIFLOWER

1 large head cauliflower for every 10 people
Salt
Lemon juice

REMOVE THE GREEN LEAVES and any black spots from the cauliflower. Trim the stem but leave the whole head intact. Place the cauliflower on a plate, rub the top with lemon juice, and salt it lightly.

Steam the cauliflower in a Chinese or vegetable steamer until tender (a pronged fork should easily pierce a large stem section). Serve the head whole and let guests cut off their own portions.

CARROTS

½ to 1 carrot per person (choose carrots with greens attached)
Salt

SCRAPE THE CARROTS and cut off the whispy ends, but leave the stems attached. Tie the carrots together at the stems.

Bring a pot of salted water to the boil and place in the carrots. Leave the greens resting over the edge of the pot and the stems just out of the water. Simmer until the carrots are tender (test with a fork), then lift out the bunch. The greens will make a nice addition to the vegetable display.

Beets

½ to 1 beet per person, depending on size
1 tablespoon sugar
Salt

CUT OFF THE BEET GREENS (eat them on another occasion), but leave 2 inches of stems attached. Cover and cook the beets in salted, sugared water until tender. Rinse the beets under cold water and slip off the skins and stems. To serve, place beets on a dark-surfaced dish. Cut 1 beet into thick slice, and place a knife in the dish so that guests can cut their own portions.

New Potatoes

3 to 4 new potatoes per person
Salt

SCRUB THE POTATOES LIGHTLY. Cover with cold salted water and bring to a boil in a covered pan. Cook until tender but not mushy.

Shrimp in their Shells

3 to 4 (or more) large shrimp in the shell per person
Salt
A generous *bouquet garni*

BRING A LARGE POT OF SALTED WATER, containing a *bouquet garni*, to the boil. Add the shrimp and boil for around 3 minutes. Drain well.

Trees of Potatoes or Shrimp

1 15-inch Styrofoam cone
Handsome leaves of kale, savoy cabbage, or mustard greens
Curly parsley
Thin florist's wire and pins
Toothpicks; bamboo skewers

TO FORM A BASE COLOR FOR THE TREE, wrap green leaves around the cone and attach them with pins and twists of wire. For the potato cone, start at the top with a row of potatoes, each attached on the end of a toothpick, then fasten on a green, wreathing line of parsley. Alternate rows of potatoes and parsley and end with potatoes. For the shrimp tree, cover the cone first with green leaves, then parsley. Attach the shrimps by pushing toothpicks into their tops and then arranging the shrimps in neat verticle lines up and down the cone. (To build an artichoke tree, a heavier form is needed. A large cone built from chicken wire and dowels driven into a solid wood base will support the weight, but a tiered, wire fruit basket can also serve to hold an array of artichokes interspersed with lemons and greenery.)

Chick Peas

1 pound chick peas (for 10 to 12 people)
Salt
A large *bouquet garni*

PLACE CHICK PEAS IN A POT, bury the *bouquet garni* in their midst, and cover with cold, salted water. Bring to the boil, let cook for 2 minutes, then turn off the heat and leave for 1 hour. Drain and cover with fresh water. Replace the *bouquet garni* in the pot and simmer the peas until tender (around 20 minutes). Drain, remove herb bundle, salt, and place in a serving dish.

ROASTED LEG OF LAMB

A 4- to 5-pound leg of lamb (for 12 to 15 people)
2 large cloves garlic, peeled
2 tablespoons finely crumbled mixed herbs (thyme, oregano,
     savory, rosemary)
Salt
¼ cup red wine
Olive oil

TRIM ALL EXCESS FAT from the lamb and place the leg in a roasting
pan. Cut each garlic clove into 6 long slivers. With a small, sharp knife,
cut deep slits about the surface of the lamb and insert a section of garlic
into each hole. Scatter the herbs over the lamb and salt abundantly.
Sprinkle the wine over the leg and then a generous coating of olive oil.
Massage the herbs and oil into and over the meat. Let the lamb sit for 30
minutes before roasting.

Preheat your oven to its highest setting. Place the lamb in the oven
and listen until you hear serious hissing and sizzling. Let the lamb carry
on in this noisy fashion for 5 minutes, then turn the heat down to 250
degrees and set a timer for 1 hour. Remove from oven and let the lamb
sit for 20 minutes before you carve it. Cut thin slices and arrange on
platters. The meat should be served cool.

SALT COD

2 pounds fileted salt cod (for 15 to 20 people)

FRESHEN THE SALT COD by covering it with cold water and letting it
sit overnight. (Change the water once during this period.) Drain well,
place in a stainless-steel pan, cover with fresh cold water, and bring to a
bare simmer. Poach the fish for 10 to 15 minutes or until the flesh flakes
easily with a fork. Lift out filets and arrange on a heated platter. This
must be served hot.

Note: Although salt cod is not to everyone's taste and often can not
be easily obtained, I mention it here for the sake of provincial
authenticity, for it surely would be the mainstay of *le Grand Aïoli* in
Provence.

Aïoli

4 large garlic cloves, peeled
1 whole egg, plus 2 egg yolks, at room temperature
¼ teaspoon salt
Freshly ground pepper
Lemon juice
Olive oil
1 teaspoon boiling water (optional)

MASH THE GARLIC to a fine pulp in a mortar. Place garlic, eggs, salt, pepper, and a good squeeze of lemon juice in the bowl of a food processor, and process until thick and pale. Add oil, a tablespoon at a time, until the mixture looks like thin mayonnaise, then continue adding oil in a small, steady stream until a thick, stiff mayonnaise forms. (Its density should support a spoon upright.) Add lemon juice to taste and adjust seasoning.   Serves 6 to 8

Note: *Aïoli* can also be made more traditionally by mounting the sauce in a mortar exactly like mayonnaise. Small mortars and processors will not be able to manage much more volume than this, so many batches will have to be made for a large crowd. If the mayonnaise is not going to be consumed shortly after it is made, stabilize each batch with 1 teaspoon of boiling water when you adjust the seasoning; in so doing, the *aïoli* can be stored, tightly covered, for up to a week.

Minted Lemon Granité

2 cups sugar
Strips of zest from 3 lemons
2½ cups water
1 cup lemon juice
½ cup orange juice
Fresh mint leaves

PLACE SUGAR, lemon zest, and 1½ cups of water in a saucepan. Bring to a gentle boil and let cook for 10 minutes. Remove from heat and cool to room temperature. Add the fruit juices and 1 cup of water, then strain through a fine sieve. Place in the refrigerator to cool.

Pour the mixture into clean ice trays and freeze until solid. Just before serving, break the ice into large sections and place in the bowl of a food processor along with 3 or 4 mint leaves. Blend until the ice is a grainy slush. Heap into chilled sherbet glasses, garnish with mint leaves, and serve.   Serves 8

Note: For a large party, start freezing blocks of lemon ice 2 weeks in advance. When they are frozen, break them up and store in plastic freezer bags. Blend the ice an hour before guests arrive and hold in a large pan in the freezer. Just before serving, break the ice up with chops of a heavy metal spoon. The very granular crunch of the ice is what you are counting on to refresh and stimulate the guests.

A SOUTHERN PIG PICKIN'

The Inspiration

. . . the ritual roasting of a whole pig that is a traditional element on so many special occasions in the South.

Have a family reunion or a Labor Day gathering, or hold a summer's church supper, and chances are that a barbecued pig or two will form the centerpiece of the meal. The roasted pig, and the fact that it is large and whole, that it is crisply gilded, that it is in a single gesture the very soul of beneficent and excessive abundance, somehow quickens any occasion and turns it into a gala affair. The pig itself creates activity, and those who tend it, who fuss and bother with the burning coals and wield the knives that slash and pick the meat, are only too aware of the importance of their position. I'm not sure just why it is that the whole roasted animal should be in most cultures the epitome of gracious hospitality, but it is so. From the biblical fatted calf slaughtered to welcome back the

A
Southern
Pig Pickin'

prodigal son on, one finds constant historical mention of whole roasted birds and piglets, of barons of beef and oxen offered for festive occasions. The North Africans slaughter a lamb for their *méchoui*; meat-poor West Africans will sacrifice a goat to celebrate. At Thanksgiving, American families must have the largest creature that will fit into their ovens, a turkey, brown upon their tables. Perhaps, as the French anthropologist Claude Lévi-Strauss says, it is an attempt to mimic the aristocratic. We do not boil our meats for entertaining, even though that is the way we could, by preserving all the meat's vitality, provide the most nutritious food. (We boil foods for invalids after all, and feed them bland, white stuffs.) But we golden roast for company; and in roasting there is destruction, for fat melts and drips away, savory juices are lost to the fire. Boiling, says Lévi-Strauss, smacks of economy and is therefore middle-class common, whereas roasting is willful, wasteful, and wantonly aristocratic.

Whether one attempts to analyze the symbolism of the occasion or not, it is true that no single entrée will draw as much dramatic attention as an entire animal laid out upon a fragrant bed of coals, with its abundant, gilded flesh waiting to be shared with friends and relatives.

Setting the Scene

The barbecued pig at a pickin' is always surrounded by the same easy dishes: cabbage slaw; beans or black-eyed peas (both of which can easily profit from being made ahead and then reheated), and hot cornbread.

Cooking the whole pig is a more complicated matter, and if it should prove too difficult, great racks of barbecued ribs can be offered in its stead and the feast will still be most delicious.

In the South, it is easy to hire a man to dig a pit and tend the cooking of the pig. (Some possess large smoking vats on wheels, which they tow about behind them to catered occasions, leaving in their highway wake the succulent odor of roasting pork.) It is also easy in the South to find a slaughterhouse which is used to dressing pigs, but the following directions will instruct the whole process from killing the pig to roasting it.

As a pig pickin' is a most casual affair, it is easiest to set a large table buffet style with platters of meat and accompanying side dishes. I like to use rustic, patchwork clothes at such a time, with simple bouquets of wild flowers centered at each table where people will place themselves to eat.

To accommodate the roasting, measure the pig, then dig a large hole that is 20 inches longer and 20 inches wider than the pig itself. The hole should be 20 inches deep at one end, with a gradual sloping to 10 inches deep at the other end. Line the pit with flat pieces of tile or smooth stones. A large grill, easily constructed of crossed pipes and covered with ¼-inch heavy mesh wire, should sit over the pit.

A source of live coals must be nearby (either a large barbecue unit or a hole in the ground will suffice to hold them). It is possible to use charcoal briquets for the fire, but good oak or hickory wood makes a more flavorful cooking heat. (You will need slightly less then half a cord of wood for the endeavor, and under no circumstances should lighter fluid be used in the roasting process, for its odor would easily penetrate the meat.)

In feeding a crowd, count ½ pound dressed pig per person. A pig loses about ⅓ of its weight in dressing, therefore a 150-pound pig will dress out to 100 pounds and feed 50 people. An 80-pound dressed pig (the smallest used for barbecuing) feeds 40 people, and a 120-pound dressed pig (as large as should be used) feeds 60 guests. Guests should arrive just as the pig has cooked from 7½ to 8 hours.

THE
MENU
(FOR 20)

Roasted Barbecued Pig

Hoppin' John

Cabbage Slaw

Skillet Cornbread

*The World's Biggest, Richest
Pecan Pie*

Iced Tea

Beer

ROASTED BARBECUED PIG

An 80- to 120-pound dressed, inspected pig

Sauce:
5 cups chili sauce
5 cups catsup
4½ cups white wine vinegar
½ cup lemon juice
⅔ cup Dijon-style mustard
⅓ cup Worcestershire sauce
4 dried red peppers, crushed
2 tablespoons salt
1 tablespoon paprika
2 tablespoons ground ginger
Freshly ground black pepper

COMBINE ALL INGREDIENTS for the sauce but the black pepper in a large, stainless-steel saucepan. Simmer for 20 minutes, stirring frequently. Grind in plenty of pepper. Makes 1 gallon of barbecue sauce.

Select a pig that is not fatty: no Poland China or Durock Jerseys, but rather a Hamshire pig with a white strap around its shoulder or a long, red pig known commonly as a Razorback. Pick a lean, straight pig with fat no thicker than ¾ inch at the shoulder.

First shoot the pig. Cut the throat from jowl to jowl, then tip the pig up and let him drain for 10 to 15 minutes. (The blood can be saved for blood sausage if so desired.) Do not let the pig get stiff and cold. Immediately have a large vat of scalding hot water available. Put the pig in and roll him around. Pluck a little of the hair to see if it is loose. The pig should be in the water 4 to 5 minutes. Beyond that, more time will make it harder for the hair to be removed. Take the pig out and scrape him with a large knife until he is pretty and white and clean.

Right above the hock bone on the hind legs is an indentation. Cut into and slice the tendons at this point. Place the ends of a 2½-foot-long dowel (traditionally called a gambling stick) into these 2 indentations. The pig can now be hung from a large branch or a sturdy clothesline. Place a tub under the pig. Gut the pig by slitting the underside from tail to throat. The intestines will fall into the tub. Loosen and pull out the remainder of the offal. Use a hose to wash down the pig until he is completely clean on the interior. Dry the pig, lower him to the ground, and place him on clean newspapers. With a heavy cleaver, cut through each rib close to the backbone. (The rib must be cut completely in two so that the animal can be flattened.) Cut through the underside of the head and then spread the pig out and press down on the backbone to smooth and level the beast. Place the gambling stick between the legs and hang and refrigerate the pig for 1 day before cooking.

Build a great bed of coals in the cooking pit. Place the pig, rib-side down, on the fire and cook for 3 hours over an intense, continuing heat. (Do not cook any longer on this side or the meat will be in danger of falling from the bones when the pig is overturned.)

Turn the pig onto its back. Pour half the barbecue sauce onto the pig and let it collect in all the small interior pockets. The pig will now cook for another 5 hours on its back, and during this period it should be often mopped and basted with more sauce. (The coals, of course, should be continuously replenished as needed).

After 5 hours on its back, the center rib section will be ready to eat (the shoulders and hams may need another 2 hours). Test the meat for doneness by pulling on and twisting the bones in the meat. When they loosen and pull out easily, the meat in that section is ready to be picked and eaten.

In the last 2 hours of cooking, not as many coals will be needed as at the beginning. The fat will now drip continuously, feeding and coaxing the coals along, but the fire should not be allowed to catch and burn the pig.

At the end of 10 hours, the pig should be entirely cooked. Remove the crackling skin and cut any remaining meat from the bones. Chop the meat into bite-sized pieces and place it into containers. Pour barbecue sauce over the meat, and let guests take home portions of both meat and crackling.

Hoppin' John

Hoppin' John is a traditional dish of North and South Carolina. Not far removed in spirit from Creole red beans and rice, this dish is often eaten on New Year's day along with fried collard greens. (The reasoning goes that if you eat greens, your pockets will be filled with dollar bills in the coming year, and if you eat beans you will have plenty of small change.) Sometimes a coin is slipped into the beans and whoever receives the portion containing the money stands to have a year of special good luck. There is no reason to use this ritual only at New Year's, however, but be sure to warn guests of the coin if you choose to use one.

4 cups dried black-eyed beans (peas)
1 hog jowl, *or* a ½-pound piece of streaky bacon
1 large onion, diced
1 large *bouquet garni* (parsley, bay leaf, thyme, celery)
1½ teaspoons salt
Freshly ground pepper
¼ teaspoon cayenne, or to taste
2 cups long-grain rice
1 large lump of butter

RINSE AND PICK OVER THE BEANS, discarding any that are withered or any small stones. Soak the beans overnight in cool, covering water. Drain well.

Add fresh cool water until the beans are covered by 1 inch. Place the hog jowl or bacon in the center, and add onion, *bouquet garni*, salt, and peppers. Cook the beans, uncovered, until tender.

Cook the rice separately in salted water. When it is just short of done (around 20 minutes), drain the rice and rinse it under hot water. Add the rice to the beans and continue cooking another 10 minutes. Taste carefully for seasoning. The consistency should be moist but not soupy. Continue to cook and reduce if necessary.

Remove the *bouquet garni*. Take out the jowl or bacon, cut it into morsels, and add the meat to the beans. (The beans can be refrigerated and reheated later after this point.) Stir in a lump of butter before serving. Serves 20

Cabbage Slaw

2 large Savoy cabbages
1 large green cabbage
2 large onions, chopped fine
6 carrots, shredded
2 green peppers, diced
⅓ cup minced parsley

Dressing:

2 cups mayonnaise
1 cup heavy cream, loosely whipped
2 tablespoons celery seeds
2 tablespoons sugar
1½ teaspoons salt
Freshly ground pepper
1 tablespoon Worcestershire sauce
3 tablespoons lemon juice
3 tablespoons white wine vinegar

BREAK THE HANDSOME OUTER GREEN LEAVES from the Savoy cabbages. Rinse them and place them in layers of damp paper toweling. Refrigerate until needed. Take the larger of the 2 Savoy heads and dig out a hollow so that the cabbage becomes a small bowl.

Core the remaining Savoy cabbage and the large green cabbage. Shred these cabbages very fine, or chop them in a food processor. Combine cabbage, onions, carrots, green peppers, and parsley in a bowl and mix well.

Make a dressing by combining mayonnaise, cream, celery seeds, sugar, salt and pepper, Worcestershire sauce, lemon juice, and vinegar. Stir until well blended and taste for seasoning. (Add more sugar if you prefer a sweeter dressing, or more acid to taste.) Stir the dressing into the chopped cabbage.

Select a very large salad bowl (a clear acrylic bowl allows the most handsome presentation). Line the bowl with the Savoy cabbage leaves, letting the leaves hang over the edge so that they provide a frilly border. Fill the hollowed-out cabbage head with slaw. Heap the remaining slaw into the cabbage-lined bowl and nestle the filled head in the center.

Serves 20

SKILLET CORNBREAD

1½ cups yellow cornmeal
2⅔ cups unbleached flour
3 tablespoons baking powder
1½ teaspoons salt
⅓ cup granulated sugar
¼ cup packed light brown sugar
4 eggs, beaten
½ cup heavy cream
3 strips bacon
1 stick unsalted butter
3 to 4 tablespoons hot water

IN A LARGE BOWL, place cornmeal, flour, baking powder, salt, and sugars and mix well. Stir in the beaten eggs and cream and let the mixture sit while preparing the bacon.

Fry the bacon in a pan. When it is just crisp, remove bacon and add the butter to the pan to melt. Crumble the bacon very fine and add it and the melted butter to the batter. Thin the batter slightly with a bit of hot water.

Preheat oven to 425 degrees.

Grease 2 round 8-inch pans or 1 longer 9 × 12-inch pan (iron skillets and molds are the most handsome) and place them in the hot oven.

Pour a bit of oil in a frying pan and, when it is hot, spoon some of the cornbread batter into the pan in an open-petaled daisy shape. When the design has set firmly, remove it with a spatula and make another flower.

Pour the remaining batter into the piping hot, greased pans and place the flowered patterns, browned side up, on top. Bake the cornbreads for around 25 minutes (test for doneness by inserting a knife blade in the center, which should come out clean). Serve from the pans.   Serves 20

The World's Biggest, Richest Pecan Pie

Crust:
3 sticks unsalted butter, cut in small chunks
1 teaspoon salt
3¾ cups all-purpose flour
1 cup ice water, approximately

Filling:
1⅓ cups (2 sticks plus 5 tablespoons) unsalted butter
2 cups light brown sugar
10 large eggs
1 teaspoon salt
2 teaspoons vanilla extract
2 tablespoons rum
1½ cups corn syrup
½ cup molasses
4 cups pecans, roughly chopped
¼ cup flour
10 ounces semisweet chocolate chips

Stiffly whipped cream, sweetened to taste with confectioners sugar
Chocolate sauce
Butterscotch and Bourbon sauce

TO PREPARE THE CRUST, place butter, salt, and flour in a bowl. Using your fingertips, work the butter into the flour rapidly until it is well blended. Sprinkle on ice water and draw the dough together into a ball. Give 3 or 4 quick kneads to the dough to ensure its smoothness, then wrap the dough and let it rest for 30 minutes. (This amount will fill a 14-inch paella pan or 3 more standard pie dishes.)

Preheat the oven to 375 degrees.

Roll out the dough and transfer it to the baking dish or dishes. Crimp a rimming border. Line the dough with heavy foil, then weight the foil down with dried beans or a large, flat lid. Bake in the oven for 10 minutes. Reduce heat to 350 degrees. Remove beans and foil and let the dough dry another 5 minutes. Cool the crust before filling.

To make the filling, cream the butter and sugar until light and lemon colored. Add eggs, 2 at a time, and stir well after each addition. Add salt, vanilla, rum, corn syrup, and molasses and blend completely.

Place the pecans in a large sieve and sprinkle them with a few drops of water. Scatter flour over the nuts and, holding the sieve over the sink, toss the nuts to coat them lightly with flour. Add pecans and chocolate chips to the filling and pour into the cooled pie crust.

Bake for 35 to 40 minutes and protect the surface with aluminum foil if it seems to be overbrowning. Test the pie for doneness by inserting a knife at its center. The knife should make a clean withdrawal, with no damp portion of filling upon it.

Serve the pie at room temperature. Just before serving, whip a quantity of cream very stiff and pipe it around the edge. Heap a mound of cream at the pie's center and drizzle over it a bit of both Chocolate and Butterscotch and Bourbon sauces.   Serves 20

CHOCOLATE SAUCE

8 ounces semisweet chocolate
¾ cup water
½ cup sugar
Pinch of salt
4 tablespoons unsalted butter
Pinch of cinnamon
1 tablespoon cognac

MELT CHOCOLATE and water together over low heat. Add sugar and salt and simmer the sauce for 5 minutes. Off the heat, stir in the butter and when it has dissolved, add the cinnamon and cognac. Serve the sauce just slightly warmed so it will be pourable.

Butterscotch and Bourbon Sauce

1 cup light corn syrup
1¾ cups packed light brown sugar
6 tablespoons butter
½ teaspoon salt
1 cup heavy cream, at room temperature
¼ cup bourbon

COMBINE CORN SYRUP, sugar, butter, and salt in a small, heavy pan and bring to a simmer. Simmer for 5 minutes. Off the heat, stir in the cream in 2 or 3 portions and then add the bourbon. Strain the sauce through a sieve. This sauce, also, must be slightly warmed so it can be poured.

Manet, *Déjeuner sur l'Herbe* (Luncheon on the Grass). Scala/Editorial Photocolor Archives.

DÉJEUNER SUR L'HERBE

The Inspiration

. . . Édouard Manet's famous painting of luncheon on the grass with its pairing of two staid, fully dressed scholar-philosophers and two demimondaines in varying states of dishabille.

The open-air picnic, or *fête Champêtre*, has always been a favorite theme for artists, but Manet was the first so-called modern painter to suggest that other than nymphs and disinterested gods attended such affairs. Staring out from the painting is a knowing, contemporary hussy who has thrown off her clothes and then carelessly piled a picnic lunch upon them. Tough as nails she sits, flaunting her tender *suprêmes* and daring you to make an issue of it. The curious element in the whole scene is that the gentleman scholars, in dark, formally clothed contrast about her, do not seem inclined even to remove their hats. To what, one wonders, can it all lead?

In 1863, the picture was refused by the Paris Salon because it so outraged both the critics and the viewing public. Hung in a salon for rejected paintings, it titillated crowds of curious viewers and reaped

Déjeuner
sur
l'Herbe

pages of virulent journalistic abuse. In gazing at the picture, I am reminded of a luncheon I once attended when I was very young, on a hot day in France. An attractive, sedate (she was a dentist, for heaven's sake) woman of a certain age suddenly addressed the company. "Do you mind," she said, "If I remove my blouse? It is so hot."

"No, of course not," everyone murmured.

Off the blouse came and there she sat for the remainder of the meal in the prettiest white brassiere one can imagine. No one would have thought a thing about it had it been a bathing suit, but the effect of the unexpected scalloping lace, the frivolous silken rosettes, was riveting. Nothing, as I recall, happened after lunch, but lunch itself seemed wickedly delicious.

Other than the nude, what strikes one most in *Déjeuner* is the still life by the side of the lady, which would make a pretty painting on its own. All ripe and sensuous pleasures are painted in her corner. There on the discarded, voluminous dress of azure polka dots is a loaf of bread, an upset basket spilling plums, peaches touched with clear vermilion, and blood-red cherries linked with stems, two by two, just waiting, waiting. . . .

Setting the Scene

Know precisely where you are going. Select an idyllic site beforehand for the picnic; do not rule out the living room.

Provide a few large straw hats, and carry the food in baskets and one large cooler. The following menu has been selected because it presents the fewest number of dishes that need to be cooled. Carry the pâté and salad greens (wrapped in several layers of paper toweling) along with the wine, in the ice chest. If the cheeses and salad solids will be eaten within an hour of leaving home, they need not be chilled. Toss the salad thirty minutes before eating, for a lukewarm and slightly wilted leaf is meant to be.

Carry as few implements as possible: certainly a fork for everyone, but only a few knives, as it is more *intime* to share. And I would make a special effort to bring real plates and glasses, cloth napkins, rather than paper picnic ware. Buy four yards of silken azure blue material (a lining fabric is cheapest), and drape it and selected lingerie informally under the picnic dishes. (Is it a white petticoat by the great brimmed hat in the picture?)

It would be nice if someone played the lute but, failing that, a tape recording of John Williams on the guitar would be lovely.

THE
MENU
(FOR 10)

Pâté of Duck and Olives

*Warm Salad with Pears and
Cracklings*

Fresh Bread

Seasoned Cheeses

Black-eyed Susan Cake

Peaches, Plums, Cherries

*Wine: a full bodied
Côtes-du-Rhône*

Pâté of Duck and Olives

2 large ducks, fresh or frozen and totally thawed
1 pound chicken breasts, boned
3 cloves garlic
4 shallots, minced
2 tablespoons cognac
1 cup red wine
1 bay leaf
20 ounces fresh spinach
1 cup black olives, pitted (preferably Calamata)
8 ounces salt pork (freeze 20 minutes before needed)
⅔ cup blanched almonds, chopped
2 eggs
3 slices firm bread, crusts removed, crumbled
¼ cup minced parsley
1 teaspoon oregano
1 teaspoon thyme
½ teaspoon allspice
Salt and freshly ground pepper
¾ pound leaflard, cut in thin barding slices

Liver Mousse: 1½ sticks unsalted butter
1 small onion, chopped
½ pound chicken livers
Salt, pepper, nutmeg

Pastry: 4½ cups all-purpose flour
1 teaspoon salt
1 pound firm unsalted butter, cut in cubes
1 teaspoon lemon juice
¾ cup ice water, approximately
1 egg yolk for glaze

CUT OFF THE DUCKS' WINGS and keep them, along with the carcasses, for stock. Reserve the livers and hearts. Remove the breasts by cutting along the breast bone and, with a sharp knife, scraping along the ribs and pulling back the flesh. Cut off the legs and salvage as much meat, minus tendons, from the thighs and back as possible. Remove all skin from both duck and chicken breasts and cut skin into narrow strips about 1 inch long. Reserve strips to make cracklings for the salad.

Slice the meat into thin strips. In a bowl, place meat, 1 crushed clove of garlic, shallots, cognac, wine, and bay leaf. Mix well and refrigerate for 2 hours, turning the meat several times during this period.

While the meat marinates, wash, stem, and cook the spinach in just the water clinging to its leaves. Refresh under cold water and wring the mass as dry as possible. Chop well and set aside.

Bring a small pot of water to the boil and plunge in the pitted olives. Let them boil for 1 minute to remove excessive salt, then drain well, press off all liquid, and chop the olives coarsely.

Dice the salt pork by criss-crossing the half-frozen fat with cuts that extend down to the rind. Cut several slices parallel to the rind to release the cubes. There should be around ¾ cup.

Butter or oil a 10-inch round, straight-sided cake pan. Preheat the oven to 350 degrees.

Drain the marinade from the duck and reserve. Remove and discard garlic and bay leaf. Either run the flesh through a meat grinder or food processor, or chop it very fine by hand (a meat cleaver best serves the process).

Combine meat, spinach, olives, salt pork, almonds, eggs, bread, herbs, spices, and generous seasonings. Add 2 pressed or minced garlic cloves and mix the ingredients well with your hands.

Line the bottom and sides of the mold with a few slices of leaflard. Place the duck mixture on top and, with wet hands, pack it down firmly. Place more strips of fat over the top of the meat. Tuck a sheet of aluminum foil loosely over the top of the mold. Place the mold in a larger baking pan and pour hot water into the pan until it reaches halfway up the sides of the mold. Bake in the oven for 1 hour.

Unmold the meat, wrap it in foil, and place it between 2 plates in the refrigerator. Weight the top plate with a 1- or 2-pound can. Leave to mellow for a day or so.

Prepare a chicken liver mousse. In a skillet, melt 4 tablespoons of butter. Cook the onion over low heat until it is soft but unbrowned. Remove the onion with a slotted spoon and, in the butter remaining in the pan, sauté the chicken and duck livers and hearts over brisk heat for around 3 minutes (a hint of pink should remain in the interiors). Thoroughly press the livers against the side of the pan, then add them to the onion. Pour the marinade liquid into the skillet, turn up the heat, and, scraping the pan constantly, let the liquid reduce to 2 tablespoons of glaze. Add glaze to the livers. Purée the livers in a food processor or blender. Season with salt, pepper, and a light scraping of nutmeg. Cover tightly and refrigerate. Just before using, cream 1 stick of butter. Add the livers and blend evenly.

For the pastry casing, prepare a rough puff pastry. Mix flour and salt in a bowl. Add the butter and work flour and butter together with the fingertips until the mixture is uniformly flaky. Add lemon juice to ice water. Sprinkle the water over the flour, adding more water if necessary, until the mixture can be neatly packed into a ball.

On a floured surface, roll the dough out to a rectangle approximately 9 by 12 inches. Fold the dough up and over into thirds. Cover the dough with plastic wrap and refrigerate for a minimum of 40 minutes. Roll out the dough and fold it, keeping the corners as square as possible, 2 more times. After each fold, refrigerate another minimal 40 minutes.

Cover the exterior bottom and sides of the mold in which the pâté was baked with lightly oiled aluminum foil. Roll out the pastry and drape it over the oiled foil. Cut the pastry evenly, so that the sides are 2 inches long. Place the mold on a baking sheet (it will bake upside down, in effect). Roll out the remaining dough over the back of a large baking tin and cut a generous, 11-inch circle. Prick the circle over with a fork and cut a hole in the center. Use the scraps to decorate what will become the lid of the pâté. Beat the egg yolk with 1 tablespoon of water and brush the surfaces of the dough. Let rest for 30 minutes before baking.

Bake in a 350 degree oven for around 30 minutes or until the pastry is gilded. Keep a particular watch on the lid. Prick and press down any bubbles that might form, and cover the quicker-browning decorations with pieces of foil. When the pastry has cooled, lift the casing off its mold and gently remove the foil.

To assemble the pâté, place the round of meat into the pastry casing. Spread the liver mousse over the top and sides. Place the lid, which should stay affixed by means of the mousse, on top. Cut into wedges to serve.   Yields 12 large portions

Warm Salad with Pears and Cracklings

2 firm pears
Olive oil
6 small eggs, *or* 12 quail eggs
1½ cups red wine
3 carrots, scraped
1 cup small lima beans, fresh or frozen
1 cup green peas, fresh if possible
10 lean bacon strips
Duck and chicken skins (see preceding recipe)
1 cup alfalfa sprouts
Watercress
Boston or Bibb lettuce
Chicory

Dressing:
Coarse salt, peppercorns
1 large clove garlic
⅓ cup white wine or honey vinegar
Fresh herbs (savory, chives, lemon thyme, hyssop), optional

PEEL AND CORE THE PEARS. Cut them into long strips about ⅓ inch thick. Place pears in a glass or stainless-steel bowl and cover with olive oil. Refrigerate the pears, covered, for from 2 to 6 hours before needed.

Hard boil the eggs. Immediately run them under cold water, then roll the eggs on a counter to lightly crack the shells. Peel and place the warm eggs in a small dish containing the red wine. Refrigerate the eggs for 2 to 6 hours before needed, and turn the eggs several times during this period so that the whites become uniformly stained.

Cut the carrots into julienne strips. Parboil or steam the carrots briefly; they should remain quite crunchy.

Cook the lima beans and peas in salted water until tender.

Fry the bacon until crisp. Drain well and crumble. Pour off the bacon fat, wipe the pan clean, then add ½ inch of oil. Heat the oil, then fry the duck and chicken skin strips until crisp. Drain well. Roll cracklings and bacon in layers of paper toweling.

To compose the dressing, place a small portion of coarse salt, a few peppercorns, and the garlic clove in a mortar. Crush until they become a paste. Add vinegar and herbs, then beat in olive oil from the pears until a pleasing vinaigrette is formed. (Taste as you go and add more acid or seasoning as needed.)

In the salad bowl, combine dressing, drained pears, carrots, lima beans, peas, and alfalfa sprouts and mix well. Place crisp, impeccably dried greens over the top. Carry the salad in this state to the picnic grounds. Before tossing, add the bacon and cracklings. Arrange the quartered eggs (or whole quail eggs) on top.   Serves 10

FRESH BREAD

1½ envelopes dry yeast
2 heaping tablespoons natural malt (as in malted milk)
2⅓ cups warm water
2 teaspoons salt
6 to 7 cups unbleached flour

A straight-edged razor blade

ADD YEAST AND MALT TO THE WARM WATER. Let sit for 5 minutes, then stir until dissolved. Add salt. Stir in approximately 4 cups of flour, or enough so that a loose, shaggy dough forms that can be turned out onto a counter. Continue adding flour and kneading until the dough no longer has a tendency to feel sticky, but at the same time, keep it as soft as possible. Knead the dough vigorously. Place the left foot back, your weight on the forward right foot, and rock into the dough with the heels of the hands until it stretches and elongates, then fold the dough back onto itself. Continue in this manner for a good 10 minutes. The dough should feel firm and elastic.

Place the dough in a lightly greased bowl, cover it with a towel, and let rise for 1 hour or until doubled in bulk.

Punch the dough down well, then form it into a perfect ball. First stretch the dough across the top of the mass and pinch and tuck a seam underneath. Repeat this process twice more which should allow the dough a certain tensile ability to remain in its rounded shape. Place the dough on an oiled baking sheet and leave to rise in a warm place for 45 minutes. A thin skin should form over the loaf during this period.

Preheat oven to 400 degrees.

Immediately before baking the bread, slash an X on the loaf, the lines of which should extend as far around the circumference as possible. Give the loaf a quick spray of water with a plant mister and place it in the hot oven. Bake for 15 minutes, spraying quickly at 5-minute intervals. Turn the oven down to 350 degrees and bake for another 40 minutes. The loaf is finished when it emits a hollow sound when thumped on its bottom with the knuckles. Place the loaf on a cake rack until cool.

SEASONED CHEESES

6 small cheeses (goat *banons*, a selection of Boursins, other small
    soft cheeses but all of a type)
¼ cup chopped parsley and chives
3 tablespoons turmeric
3 tablespoons paprika
3 tablespoons black peppercorns, coarsely cracked
⅓ cup ground nuts (walnuts or unblanched almonds)

SMALL CHEESES rolled in an assortment of colorful and flavorful
coatings are a current vogue in chic Parisian *fromageries*. Sometimes each
cheese is sitting on a grape leaf atop a straw cheese drainer, or the cheeses
might be presented in a slatted wooden carton as a gift assortment.
Simply roll one cheese in each herb or spice until it is thoroughly covered
in its respective coating. Leave 1 cheese plain. Cover with plastic wrap
and refrigerate. Remove cheeses from the refrigerator 1 hour before
needed so that they can mellow. (Less time will be needed on a very
hot day.)

BLACK-EYED SUSAN CAKE

2 tablespoons unsalted butter
2 large peaches, medium ripe
2 tablespoons lemon juice
2 to 2½ cups fresh blueberries
1⅓ cups all-purpose flour, sifted before
    measuring
1 teaspoon dry yeast
Pinch of salt
1 teaspoon grated lemon zest
3 large eggs
¾ cup sugar
1 tablespoon lemon juice

Glaze: ⅔ cup sugar
⅓ cup water
2 tablespoons lemon juice
⅓ cup peach preserves, sieved
2 tablespoons light rum

USING ALL THE BUTTER, grease a 10-inch springform pan. Cut a round of kitchen parchment or brown-paper sacking to fit the bottom of the mold. Place it in the bottom and butter the top of the paper also.

Peel the peaches by plunging them briefly in boiling water. Slip off the skins and cut them, against the pit, into wedges ½ inch thick at the wider edge. Toss peaches in lemon juice. Arrange slices on the buttered paper to form a daisy pattern. Fill the daisy's center with densely packed blueberries. Place more berries around the outer edge of the flower and extending to the mold's sides. Set aside.

Preheat the oven to 350 degrees.

Mix flour, yeast, salt, and lemon zest in a bowl.

Place eggs, sugar, and lemon juice in the metal bowl of a mixer or, if using a hand mixer or whisk, in a copper egg-beating bowl or other rounded metal dish that can be placed directly over gentle heat. Allow the eggs to warm slightly as you beat them, and lift the bowl off the heat as necessary so the eggs do not cook. Beat the warmed eggs by machine or hand until they are thick and voluminous and the batter forms a ribbon. Gently fold the flour into the eggs in 3 or 4 portions. Do not overwork, as it is necessary to maintain the volume of the eggs. Pour the batter over the fruit and bake in the oven for about 45 minutes.

While the cake bakes, prepare a glazing syrup. Place all ingredients except rum in a saucepan and let simmer until thickened (about 15 minutes). Stir in rum.

Unmold the cake bottom-side up onto a platter and, while it is still warm, pour the syrup evenly over the patterned surface.   Serves 10

Seducing an Audience

THE
DINNER
OF
SEDUCTION

The Inspiration

. . . at this point the reader will have to insert his or her own provocation.

However, in order to practice the fine drama of culinary seduction, it is best initially to make a few assumptions about the players in the play. As I am a woman, I shall plot this from a female standpoint, though there is no reason why the whole procedure should not be successful in reverse.

First we must assume a certain sophistication in both partners. Now there is a perverse vision of love and food that seems to have entered our collective imaginations placed there most probably by the movie *Tom Jones*. In that film (adapted with a certain artistic leeway), strapping young Tom, who has just rescued the Widow Waters from a villainous attack, is seated with her in an inn, at a table laden with food. Gazing always into each other's eyes, they gnaw on bones; they exchange bites; they savage

Caravaggio, *Bacchus*. Scala/Editorial Photocolor Archives

THE
DINNER
OF SEDUCTION

ripe fruit, their feet entwining beneath the table while wanton juices from the pears drip down their chins. A sensual scene to be sure, but one in reality that would more likely happen after seduction, when two love-sated people who know each other well and care less how they look assuage their famished appetites.

In *Tom Jones* the book, we learn what really happened. The Widow Waters connives over dinner to seduce unknowing Tom with her whole "artillery of love." Her weapons in what Fielding calls this "war" were practiced and considerable. First from her bright blue eyes flash two pointed ogles, but they harmlessly spend their force on a piece of beef which Tom is lifting to his mouth. Next she draws from her bosom a deadly sigh so soft, so sweet, so tender that it surely would have pierced Tom's heart had it not been driven from his ears by a gurgle of ale that he was busily pouring into his cup.

Enraged at her losses, Mrs. Waters takes the measure of her man and, realizing that food has won, waits to resume the attack until after dinner. Only after the dishes are cleared, after a volley of disarming smiles and dimples, does the hero begin to sense her message. As a final shot, the lady carelessly lets drop the napkin from her bodice and "unmasks the royal battery"; then is the heart of Mr. Jones finally captured.

Well, perhaps it was worth it, but it would have been so much *easier* had both parties been more equally matched in their sophistications. At least Mrs. Waters did not have to cook the dinner, but I for one would not wish to waste my time and culinary talents preparing the following meal for a self-proclaimed "steak-and-potato" man, for instance. What a doomed effort. Furthermore, with a gustatory range that limited, is there reason to hope that his amatory grasp would be any wider?

Setting the Scene

The following menu, with its choice of main courses, is conceived in such a manner that it allows the seducer/cook to offer richly inflaming, elegant I-cared-enough-to-do-this-for-you dishes, but not at the expense of last-minute exertion. As care is taken to preserve the cook's strength, so too is careful attention paid to the amount of food offered in each serving, for one should not allow the seductee to overexert him or herself eating in a wasteful expense of primal energies. (As the food should be light, so also should be the consumption of alcohol, which as we know, promoteth desire but taketh away the performance thereof.)

It is hardly necessary to point out that the menu contains within itself as many ingredients as possible that are reputed to be aphrodisiacs: caviar, eggs, pepper, cayenne, spices, nuts, seafood, chocolate. This should not be explained to the guest, but rather allowed to enter the conscience subliminally.

At the occasion's setting, either no evidence should be given of intent, or every evidence. The current sensibilities of romance, all pink and peach and lace and roses, are more female than male, but I do not think a strong man should be threatened by the obvious, and a woman will only be more titillated when taken on her own illusionary terms.

Have the caviar chilled and the toast points, wrapped in a napkin, warming in the oven. Know the main-course recipe intimately and note at which points the dish can be stayed in preparation. Greens should be washed and chilling; there should be an optional cheese or two in case you need more time to dawdle. Have a subtle programing of music, moving from the austere to the unbridled on the phonograph. And then my little pepperpot, my pretty pattypan, turn down the lights. . . .

THE
MENU
(FOR 2)

Caviar on ice, with Parsley, Lemon Wedges, and Warm Toast Points

Champagne

EITHER
Seafood Sausages with Rice and Cucumbers
OR
Breast of Duck in a Crêpe, with Peppercorns and Crusted Potatoes

Green Salad

Cheese (if you wish to prolong the meal)

White Chocolate Mousse with Bittersweet Chocolate Sauce

Coffee (prepare extra so it can be iced, later)

Eau-de-Vie (Poire or Framboise)

Cigars

Seafood Sausages

Generous ½ pound very fresh shrimp, weighed
    after shelling (keep the shells)
1 egg
⅓ cup shelled pistachios
1 small truffle (optional)
¾ cup heavy cream, well chilled
1 teaspoon salt
Pepper, nutmeg
Minced parsley

Stock: Head and carcass of any non-oily fish, such as
    trout or flounder
1 small onion, sliced
1 carrot, sliced thin
1 clove garlic, slightly crushed
1 bay leaf
3 or 4 stems of parsley
1 cup white wine
Salt
2 cups water
½ lemon

Sauce: 1 stick chilled, unsalted butter, cut in chunks
2 tablespoons flour
Fish stock
Shrimp peelings
1 to 1½ cups heavy cream
1 tablespoon tomato paste
Cayenne
Salt and pepper

Cooked rice as an accompaniment

Lightweight aluminum foil

PREPARE A FISH STOCK as the base for the sauce. Rinse the fish head and carcass, making sure that no dark portions of blood remain attached. Cut into several pieces. Place fish, onion, carrot, garlic, herbs, wine, a very light salting, and water in a stainless-steel pan. Squeeze in the juice from the lemon half and throw in the rind also. Place pan over medium heat and bring to the boil. Immediately skim off any gray foam and coagulated protein that rise to the surface. Reduce heat to the barest

simmer, cover the pan, and cook for 30 minutes. Strain the stock through a sieve into a bowl, pressing the bones and vegetables lightly. Pour the stock, except for the last 2 or 3 sediment-filled tablespoons, into a pan and reduce to 2 measured cups.

Prepare the sauce base. In a heavy saucepan, melt 2 tablespoons of butter. Whisk in flour and continue whisking over very low heat for 2 minutes. Pour in the fish stock and raise the heat to medium. Let the sauce simmer for 10 minutes, then carefully draw a spoon across the surface and lift off the fine covering crust. Add shrimp shells and continue simmering for 15 minutes, but stir frequently to keep the sauce from scorching. Pour the sauce into a sieve and press down firmly to extract all the essence possible. Discard shells and debris. (The sauce base can be refrigerated at this point for a day then mounted with cream and butter while the sausages are cooking.)

Place the sauce base back in a pan and stir in 1 cup of cream. Add tomato paste and a sensible dash of cayenne. Heat the sauce but do not allow to boil. Whisk in the remaining butter in 2 or 3 portions and taste carefully for seasoning. Add salt if necessary, perhaps a bit of lemon juice or more cayenne as needed. There should be a slight piquancy to the sauce but not so much as to distract from the delicacy of the dish. The sauce should also be of light pouring consistency. Thin with additional cream if necessary, so that the sauce can float out to the rim of the serving plate. (Any leftover sauce should be reheated over hot water with great care so no separation occurs.)

To make the sausages, pat the shrimp as dry as possible. Purée shrimp and egg together in a food processor, or use the more classic method and pound in a sturdy mortar to a fine paste. Press the flesh through a heavy sieve (the flat drum sieve or *tamis* is the easiest to use) to strain out any fibrous filaments that would keep the forcemeat from being gossamer smooth.

Place the forcemeat in a small bowl and press plastic wrap directly down over the shrimp so that no air reaches the flesh. Refrigerate from a minimum of 1 hour to overnight.

Place the pistachios in a small pan, cover with water, and bring to a boil. Turn off the heat and let the nuts sit for 5 minutes. Strain out the nuts and place them in an old kitchen towel. Rub briskly until the skins slip away, then chop roughly and set aside. (The optional truffle should be cut into very small dice.)

Preheat the oven to 350 degrees.

Just before the sausages are to be composed, tear off 4 sheets of lightweight aluminum foil, around 10 inches long. Butter one entire side of each sheet. Fill a roasting pan with water 2 inches deep and place in the oven.

Whip ½ cup of very cold cream until it is the consistency of sludge; that is, it should move heavily in the bowl. Remove the forcemeat from the refrigerator and gradually but rapidly work in ¼ cup of plain cream with a heavy wooden spoon. Stir in pistachios, truffle, salt, pepper, and 2 or 3 scrapings of nutmeg. Fold in the whipped cream.

Dividing the forcemeat between the 4 squares of buttered foil, place spoons of the mixture on one long edge of the paper, leaving 2 inches free at either side. Roll up the foils neatly but not overly tight, and twist the foil at each end so that the forcemeat is well enclosed in its casing. Immediately place the sausages in the hot water and let them poach in the oven for a good 20 minutes. Remove and unwrap 1 sausage. If it is not firm to the touch, rewrap and poach another 5 to 10 minutes. (The water in the pan should not be allowed to boil.)

Lift out the sausages, unwrap one end slightly, and tip them over a bowl so that any poaching water can drain away. Place a sausage on a warm dinner plate, coat it lightly with sauce, and sprinkle with parsley. Allow more sauce to cover the entire plate to its rim. Arrange a mound of rice to one side of the sausage, and fan 2 cucumbers on the other side. Serve immediately. Makes 4 servings

Note: The sausages can be poached ahead of time and gently reheated later in more poaching water. If only 2 sausages are used, refrigerate the other 2 still in their foil for another occasion.

POACHED CUCUMBERS

1 large cucumber, preferably burpless
3 tablespoons butter
Salt and pepper
Minced parsley

PEEL THE CUCUMBER and cut it in half lengthwise. Spoon out the seeds and cut the lengths into 2½-inch sections. Trim and round the sections into ovals. Bring a pot of salted water to the boil and add the cucumbers. Simmer for 4 minutes or until they just begin to soften. Strain the cucumbers, then place them back in the pot.

Five minutes before needed, add butter, seasoning, and a sprinkling of parsley and heat gently.   Serves 3 to 4

BREAST OF DUCK IN A CRÊPE WITH PEPPERCORNS

1 large duck, fresh or frozen, thawed (Concord
   brand is excellent)
Salt
2 tablespoons red wine vinegar
⅓ cup red wine
1 bay leaf
1 clove garlic, lightly crushed
2-inch strip of orange peel
5 tablespoons unsalted butter
1½ cups heavy cream
1 teaspoon green peppercorns (preserved in
   natural juices or water)
Black pepper
Finely minced parsley

Crêpes:
2 rounded tablespoons flour
Large pinch of salt, pepper
1 egg
1 tablespoon butter, melted
⅓ cup milk, approximately

REMOVE THE BREASTS FROM THE DUCK. Cut off both wings at their joints. Remove the wishbone by locating it immediately at the opening of the breast cavity and running a sharp knife along its outline. Pry the flesh away from the bone with your fingers, cut any attaching tendons with a knife, then pull the bone out. (The wishbone of a duck is smaller and tougher than a chicken's, and horseshoed in shape.) Cut down one side of the central breast as close to the bone as possible. Scrape the breast section away from the rib cage and pull it off. Leave the fat skin attached, but trim it neatly. Criss-cross the skin with cuts. Rub the breasts with salt and put them into a bowl. Add vinegar, wine, bay leaf, garlic, and orange peel. Cover, refrigerate, and leave to marinate for 24 hours.

For the crêpes, place flour, salt, and 2 or 3 grinds of pepper in a mixing bowl. Combine egg, butter, and milk. Slowly whisk the liquid into the flour until the mixture is smooth. Cover and set aside for 30 minutes.

Lightly butter a crêpe or omelet pan. Give the batter a stir. When the pan is hot, lift it off the heat and over the batter bowl. Pour in a large ladle of batter, swirl the pan, and quickly tip the excess back into the bowl. Place crêpe over the heat and, when it has lightly browned, turn it over briefly and let a few brown spots appear on its other side. Slide the crêpe onto an ovenproof dish, wipe the pan with paper toweling, and make the remaining crêpes. (A few drops of water can be added to the batter if it seems too thick.) Cover the crêpes and set aside. Reheat briefly in foil while the duck is cooking. You will have around 4 8-inch crêpes. Eat the 2 extras to keep up your strength.

Remove the breasts from the marinade and pat them dry. Remove garlic, bay leaf, and orange peel and reserve the marinade.

Heat 2 tablespoons of butter in a sauté pan. When hot, place in the breasts, skin-side down. Sauté for around 8 minutes, then turn the breasts over and cook another 4 to 8 minutes, depending on how rare you like your duck. There should be at least a pale rose color at the interior. Do not hesitate to run a knife into the center to examine color and juices.

When the duck is cooked, lift the breasts onto a pan and place them in the warming oven to rest and in the process to tenderize somewhat. (The potatoes, crêpes, and dinner plates should also be warming.)

Pour off the fat from the sauté pan. Add the marinade and, scraping the bottom of the pan with a wooden spatula to incorporate the tasty caramelizations, let the wine cook over brisk heat until almost evaporated. Add the cream and boil until it reduces by half. Off the heat, whisk in remaining butter, the peppercorns, salt, and pepper to taste. Quickly wrap each duck breast in a crêpe, place it on a heated plate, and pour half the sauce over it. Add a light sprinkling of minced parsley and serve at once.

CRUSTED POTATOES

1 clove garlic, lightly crushed
2 to 3 all-purpose potatoes
Salt and pepper
Hot milk
3 tablespoons grated Gruyère cheese
3 tablespoons fine, dry bread crumbs
Butter shavings

RUB THOROUGHLY 2 individual or 1 11-inch gratin dish with the garlic clove. Discard the clove and coat the pans with butter.

Peel the potatoes and cut them into very thin slices around ⅛ inch thick. Pat the potatoes dry with paper toweling. Spread the potatoes in the dishes and season with salt and pepper. Pour hot milk over the potatoes just until they are covered. Mix cheese and crumbs and sprinkle over the surface. Place 3 or 4 thin shavings of butter over the crumbs.

Forty minutes before the duck is started, place the potatoes in a preheated 375-degree oven and let them bake. Turn the heat down to warm and let potatoes remain in the oven (along with dinner plates, crêpes, and duck breasts) until the sauce is completed.

White Chocolate Mousse with Bittersweet Chocolate Sauce

	3 ounces bittersweet chocolate

3 ounces bittersweet chocolate
9 ounces white chocolate (choose 3-ounce bars like Lindt or Tobler)
¼ cup sugar
4 egg yolks
1 stick unsalted butter, cut in bits
⅔ cup heavy cream

Sauce: 6 ounces *extra* bittersweet chocolate, if possible
2 tablespoons sugar
Salt
2 tablespoons unsalted butter, cut in pieces
1 teaspoon cognac, *or* 2 teaspoons intense coffee

SELECT 2 3- OR 4-INCH SOUFFLÉ CUPS AS MOLDS. Cut circles of wax paper to fit the bottom interiors.

Place a sheet of wax paper on a small baking sheet (attach it by rubbing a bit of butter under the paper). Trace the 2 circles on the wax paper with a pen. Lightly oil the molds and place in the paper rounds.

For decoration, melt bittersweet chocolate over warm water. After it has cooled slightly, put the chocolate in a pastry bag with a very small tip or a paper cone, and trace concentric swirls of chocolate over the 2 marked circles on the tray. Let these harden and cool. (Any leftover chocolate can be added to the sauce.)

Melt the white chocolate with half the cream. Beat sugar and egg yolks together until very thick. Pour in the melted chocolate and return to gentle heat. Stir briefly over low heat until the mixture appears very smooth. (White chocolate is sometimes difficult to work with, but it should eventually come smooth. Beating with an electric hand mixer helps.)

Off the heat, add the butter and let it melt into the chocolate. Let the mixture cool until slightly chilled, then whip remaining cream until thick but not stiff, and fold it into the chocolate. Fill 4-inch molds half full, 3-inch molds almost full (this mousse is extremely rich). Pour remaining mousse into another bowl to chill for another occasion. Cover with plastic wrap and place in the freezer overnight.

Prepare the sauce. Break the extra bittersweet chocolate into bits, add any chocolate leftover from making swirls, and place in a small, heavy pan. Add sugar and a few grains of salt and just cover with water.

Melt over very low heat, then let simmer for 2 minutes, stirring constantly.

Off the heat, whisk in butter and cognac or coffee. Let cool. Just before using, thin the chocolate with a bit of hot water until it is a light pouring consistency.

To unmold mousses, dip the bottoms of the molds in hot water and run a knife around the edges. Turn the mousse, which will never quite freeze solid, out onto a serving plate and remove wax paper. Peel the paper away from a chocolate swirl and place the design on the top of each mousse. Float chocolate sauce around the mousse and out to the rim of the plate.   Serves 8

EAU-DE-VIE

Fruited *eaux-de-vie*—pear, raspberry, prune, and so forth—are correctly served chilled (place the bottle in the refrigerator the night before), and in iced glasses. Because this involves a certain amount of bother (not *that* much really, but all the same . . .), use the excuse to prepare just one serving and share it. Have a supply of crushed ice on hand. Choose a large brandy snifter and a pretty glass bowl in which it can sit surrounded by ice. Carry the *eau-de-vie*, the bowl filled with ice, and the brandy glass to table. Place a large spoonful of ice in the snifter and swirl it round and round until the glass is very cold. Imbed the glass in the crushed ice and pour in a very small portion of liquor. Sip it slowly.

CIGARS

A good cigar can be offered in an intimate setting to either a man (for it compliments his masculinity), or a woman (for in making the overtly masculine custom hers, she can do so privately with a certain rakish and suggestive charm not possible in public). The etiquette of smoking, by the way, was an art in which the writer Colette felt women should be trained. The gauche and awkward Gigi was coached by her worldly Aunt Alicia. "You shall have an Egyptian cigarette with your coffee," she said, "on condition that you do not wet the end of your cigarette, and that you don't spit out specks of tobacco—going '*ptu, ptu.*'"

Choose a good, aged cigar of middling length and width. Cigars are meant to be kept in a humidor at a moist 70 percent humidity so they will burn slowly. Your cigars for this evening, however, should be deliberately mistreated. Carefully open them and let them dry for a day, then close them back up so no one can tell. When one is meant to be lighted, unwrap it again. "Oh," you exclaim, "how careless of me. This is too dry, you must let me fix it for you."

Take up the cigar and, with a sharp knife, cut off a small portion of paper plug from the smoking end so the cigar can draw. Then, with a delicate tongue, lick the cigar all over to restore its suppleness. Light a long match or hold a lighter under the cigar and run the tip of the flame up and down the cigar's length to heat it.

If you are a man, put the cigar in your mouth and, turning and turning it, hold the flame to the cigar until the entire end is alight and burning evenly. Hand it to the woman. If you are a woman, put the cigar in the man's mouth and let him turn it while you hold the fire.

"Ah, Gigi," says Aunt Alicia, the old seductress, ". . . remind me to teach you how to choose cigars. Once a woman understands the tastes of a man, cigars included, and once a man knows what pleases a woman, they may be said to be well matched."

BREAKFAST THE MORNING AFTER

...Continued

I f ever there was an author who understood the voluptuous potential of entwining food and love it was Colette, and a good deal about the subject can be learned by perusing her writings. Certainly she would have approved of making every effort to sustain an ambiance conducive to seduction. One of her most sensual scenes occurs in *The Ripening Seed*, when an older woman prepares to seduce a chaste young man:

> Mme. Dalleray was not expecting him, or so it seemed, for he found her reading. He felt assured of his welcome, however, when he saw the studied half-light in the *salon* and noticed the almost invisible table from which rose a pervasive aroma of slow-ripening peaches, of red cantaloup melon cut in slices the shape of crescent moons, and of black coffee poured over crushed ice.

BREAKFAST
THE MORNING
AFTER

(Note the perfection of the food chosen for the imminent occasion: cold, not hot coffee, with its stimulation of caffeine but not its sleep-inducing warmth; the energizing sugars of the fruits; the fruits themselves particularly moist and lush. . . .)

In the semi-autobiographical *Claudine* novels, Colette often equates the growing sensual awareness of her nubile, precocious young heroine to the food the girl loves: truffles, the insides of the tails of artichokes, chocolates, bananas, for example. "By buying them ripe and letting them rot just a little, bananas are sheer heaven, like eating Liberty velvet!" enthuses Claudine.

Or truffles. "I was eating a little patty with truffles that would have consoled a widow the day after her bereavement."

Claudine's friend Luce, the mistress of a wealthy older man, confides: "But he gives me money, too, that I hide under a pile of chemises and, most of all, oh! most of all, sweets and pastries and little birds to eat. And even better than that, champagne at dinner."

I have no doubt but that Colette would also agree on the necessity of a certain culinary sophistication in a lover, or at least on the predisposition toward it. ("Beware," she counseled young men, "of young women who love neither wine nor truffles nor cheese nor music.") And when Claudine finally meets Reynaud, her world-wise seducer, he knows just how to take the young girl's measure:

Renaud, sitting opposite me, had shaky hands and moist temples. A little moan of covetousness escaped me, aroused by the trail of scent left by a passing dish of shrimps.

"Some shrimps too? Well, well! How many?"

"How many? I've never discovered how many I could eat. A dozen to begin with, and after that we'll see."

"And to drink, what? Beer?"

I made a face.

"Wine? No. Champagne? Asti Spumante?"

I flushed with greed.

"Oh! *Yes!*"

Now champagne and truffles and certain other foods have long been the tools of extravagant seducers. A chef I used to know in Paris courted his wife-to-be with baskets of green beans in which he slyly secreted whole *foie gras* and fresh truffles. And I once observed, at a fashionable restaurant, an elderly *roue* bring an innocent, skittish young woman completely to heel with raspberries crushed and strained and stirred into champagne.

In the end however it must be admitted that it is, in a given time and place, the suggestibility of certain foods upon susceptible minds and not their questionable aphrodisiacal effects (which could be attained a hundred ways more cheaply) that must be reckoned with and used. A clever would-be lover, thankful that tradition long established has infused these culinary aids with powerful mystiques, will use them blatantly and trust the battle is half won.

Setting the Scene

The following breakfast menu is organized to be adaptable on a sliding scale of need and expectations. Have on hand fruit, eggs, oysters, chilled champagne, freshly squeezed orange juice (never mind the loss of vitamins just this once), prebaked coffee cake, extra coffee made the night before. If the morning parting is necessarily rushed, quickly heat the coffee (providing it wasn't iced and polished off at midnight) in a *bain-marie*; warm the coffee cake in the oven, and pour out some orange juice.

If there is time for a more leisurely breakfast, add scrambled eggs, toast, and a pretty bowl of fruit to the menu.

If the whole morning stretches before one and all signs point to a renewal of interest in the previous night's Entertainment, gird up with the oyster dish and fortify the orange juice with champagne.

THE
MENU
(FOR 2)

Freshly Squeezed Orange Juice

Coffee

Coffee Cake

*Scrambled Eggs with Herbs
and Sour Cream*

Toast

Sliced Fruit

Oysters Florentine

Champagne

FRESHLY SQUEEZED ORANGE JUICE

PLACE 2 LARGE WINE GOBLETS in the freezer.

Have the orange juice, preferably from California navals, squeezed, strained, and refrigerated in a tightly covered container. Taste the juice and add a bit of sugar if it is at all undersweet. If you have some grenadine, a small spoonful added to the juice will intensify its flavor and color. If champagne is to be added, mix 1 part juice to 2 parts champagne and serve in chilled glasses.

COFFEE CAKE

4 eggs, separated, plus 2 egg yolks, at room temperature
1 cup confectioners sugar
1 teaspoon vanilla extract
1 cup all-purpose flour, sifted
1 teaspoon cinnamon

Pastry bag and nozzle

PREHEAT THE OVEN TO 350 DEGREES.

Butter and lightly flour a baking sheet, and trace a 10-inch circle on the sheet.

Place 6 egg yolks, ½ cup sugar, and vanilla in a bowl and beat until extremely thick. (The eggs should be so firm that they mound and stay stiffly in shape when dropped from a beater.) Gently fold in the sifted flour.

Beat the egg whites and, as they start to mound, gradually add ¼ cup of sugar. Continue to beat the whites until they are stiff and glossy, but do not allow them to overdry. Fold the whites into the yolks.

Mix the cinnamon into the remaining sugar.

Spoon one-third of the voluminous batter into a large pastry bag with a plain nozzle. Set aside.

Pour out another one-third of the batter onto the baking sheet and gently smooth it into the 10-inch circle with a rubber spatula. Sprinkle with one-third of the cinnamon sugar.

Scrape the remaining batter onto the top of the cake and smooth it out. Sprinkle again with one-third of the cinnamon sugar.

With the batter in the pastry bag, pipe a design on top of the cake. Make 4 or 5 rows of small parallel lines in a mock-basket effect for the center portion (allow for some expansion of the dough), then swirl fat scallops of batter around the edge.

Sprinkle the remaining cinnamon sugar over the surface.

Bake in the oven for 30 minutes or until a cake tester, inserted in the center, comes out clean. This cake may be cooled, wrapped in foil, and reheated before serving, but it should be served warm.   Serves 6 to 8

Scrambled Eggs with Herbs and Sour Cream

5 to 6 eggs
Salt and pepper
1 large tablespoon finely minced fresh herbs (certainly parsley
     and chives or green onions; savory or chervil if possible)
1 clove garlic, peeled
3 tablespoons unsalted butter
2 to 3 tablespoons sour cream, at room temperature

PLACE 2 DINNER PLATES in the warming oven along with the coffee cake.

Break the eggs into a bowl. Add salt, pepper, and herbs. Spear the garlic clove onto a fork and beat the eggs with the fork until well blended. Remove and discard the garlic (which will have added only the most delicate uplift of flavor).

Melt butter in a double boiler or in a pan over hot but not boiling water, and add the eggs. Stir continuously as the eggs cook and thicken. (Using this method, eggs will take 3 times as long to cook as a quick scramble in a frying pan, but the results are so much better.) Scrape the side and bottom of the pan thoroughly and if large portions of egg start coagulating, lift the pan away from the heat source immediately and beat out the lumps with a whisk. The eggs should slowly evolve into an unctuous custard, with no clotted curd consistency.

Just when the eggs have cooked (they will still move thickly), stir in the sour cream, which will stop the cooking process just at the moment of the egg's perfection. Spoon the eggs onto the heated plates and eat at once with toast.   Serves 2 to 3

Oysters Florentine

10 ounces fresh spinach
4 tablespoons unsalted butter
1 tablespoon flour
1 cup milk
Salt, pepper, nutmeg
1 bay leaf
4 tablespoons grated Parmesan cheese
Cayenne
1 dozen oysters in the shell (or use shucked oysters and
    construct this dish in a gratin)
Rock salt
Lemon wedges

BREAK AND TEAR BACK THE STEMS of the spinach and wash well. Place spinach in a large pot, salt it lightly, and cook over high heat in just the water clinging to the leaves. Stir constantly and, when the spinach is limp, drain and rinse it with cool water. Squeeze the leaves as hard as possible to extract all moisture, then chop them finely.

Melt 3 tablespoons of butter in a frying pan and let it turn nut brown. Immediately add the spinach, stir for 30 seconds, and set aside.

In a small heavy pan, melt remaining butter. Whisk in the flour and stir over low heat for 1 minute. Whisk in milk, salt, pepper, and a scraping of nutmeg. Add the bay leaf and let the sauce simmer for 15 minutes. Stir frequently to avoid scorching. Remove bay leaf, add 2 tablespoons of grated cheese and enough cayenne so that the sauce is distinctly piquant.

Open the oysters (letting them sit for 5 minutes in tonic water eases the process), and pour the contents of the shells into a pan. Let the oysters cook over very low heat until the edges curl. (Do not allow them to boil.)

Scrub and rinse the deeper halves of the shells, and steady them in a roasting pan on a bed of rock salt. Smooth spinach into each shell and top with an oyster. Season with salt and pepper. Spoon cheese sauce over the oysters, and sprinkle the remaining cheese on top. (Note: at this point, the dish can be covered and refrigerated overnight.)

Heat a broiler then let the oysters warm and brown. Serve very hot and accompany with lemon wedges.   Serves 2 to 3

Experimenting with Entertaining Patterns

THE BISTRO

The Inspiration

. . . the golden bistros of France.

Some of my favorite restaurants are small bistros that provide the middle link between the formal old-guard palaces of *haute cuisine* and the very informal workingman's restaurants. With names like *Chez Camille* and *Chez Julius,* they are often established, family-run institutions, with faithful local patrons who visit them frequently. In the bistro you find a simple style of cooking, with Grandmother's dishes at the fore. Soups and stews, ragoûts, and simple grills are often served, and some bistros specialize in the dishes of a certain province so that one can go, say, to an Alsatian bistro and find all the good local dishes of that region.

As there is a certain style of food to be expected, so also is there a typical bistro setting. I think of old polished woods or speckled *faux bois* on the walls; a menu chalked upon a slate; mirrors everywhere; geraniums in pots; checkered tablecloths; impeccable white napkins; lace curtains hung from lustrous brass railings at the windows; closely placed tables; waiters with starched aprons doubled about their waists.

The bistro can be chic and elegant or unpretentiously common, but its smallness

asserie Lipp. Paris, France. FPG/Farrel Grehan

173

THE
BISTRO

makes it always intimate. It is the "arty,
tarty" restaurant where Colette the author,
thinly disguised as a greedy Claudine
hungry for love and dozens of shrimp,
falls in love with an older man: "We were
sitting at a little table against a pillar. To
my right, under a panel daubed
tempestuously with naked Bacchantes, a
mirror assured me that I had no ink on my
cheek, that my hat was on straight and
that my eyes were dancing above a mouth
red with thirst, perhaps with a little
fever . . . ." It is the kind of place that I
suppose Proust remembered when, in *The
Past Recaptured,* he recalls "the rosy glow
of eventide on the flower-covered wall of
a rustic restaurant, the feeling of hunger,
the yearning for women, the pleasant
sensation of luxury . . . ."

Setting the Scene

The informality of the bistro gives rise to a small entertaining pattern that guests always enjoy, and that is to offer a varied selection of foods for either the first course or, as is the case in the following menu, for dessert. If there is room enough in the dining room, I like to wheel a cart in and serve people as they sit at table. Failing enough space, one can simply park the cart and let guests serve themselves. (If one wished to have a selection of *hors d'oeuvre variés* for a first course, one might offer dishes of grated carrots in a highly garlicked vinaigrette; mushrooms or fennel à la grecque; a sweet onion salad; grated celery root rémoulade; boiled eggs en gelée; cold grilled eggplant with herbs and olive oil; sliced tomatoes and fresh basil; slices of sausage-stuffed peppers. All of these, with their similar sauces, can mingle successfully upon a plate. Follow this with a simple main course and a very rich dessert.)

The pattern of the following meal is one of imposed virtue followed by profound gluttony. A modest vegetarian main course is offered, followed by even more greens in the form of a salad, and then by healthy cheeses. It is important to control bread in the first portion of the meal for, particularly if it is good homemade bread, guests must not be allowed to fill themselves on it. No hint should be given about the desserts so that, when they are finally wheeled in, people will be surprised and delighted. The psychology of the evening should now be perfect, for having eaten so lightly and judiciously, guests will feel themselves positively entitled to all the sweets they want, with no attendant guilt.

A hint of bistro aura is easy to attain. Display a framed menu or write out small cards for each place setting. Use geraniums, old lace, and rustic pottery. (For more ideas, see the Bistro setting on page 170.) Dim the lights and put a supply of French songs on the phonograph: Edith Piaf certainly, and any of those grand ladies like Mistinguette or Lys Guity from the French music halls.

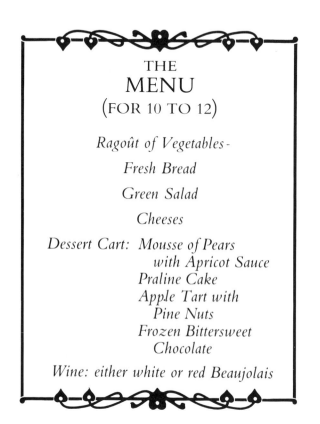

THE
MENU
(FOR 10 TO 12)

Ragoût of Vegetables-

Fresh Bread

Green Salad

Cheeses

*Dessert Cart: Mousse of Pears
with Apricot Sauce
Praline Cake
Apple Tart with
Pine Nuts
Frozen Bittersweet
Chocolate*

Wine: either white or red Beaujolais

Ragoût of Vegetables

3 large heads of Boston lettuce
Juice of 2 lemons
5 large artichokes
20 ounces pearl onions
4 to 5 large carrots
½ pound snow peas
4 medium zucchini
8 ounces firm, medium-sized button mushrooms
1 pound asparagus
15 large cloves garlic, peeled
2 cups heavy cream
1 stick plus 3 tablespoons unsalted butter, cut into chunks
Bouquet garni
4 to 5 cups lightly salted, homemade veal or chicken stock, fat
    free
Salt and pepper
⅓ cup minced fresh herbs (parsley, chives, a bit of tarragon, or
    parsley)

BRING A LARGE, STAINLESS-STEEL POT of salted water to the boil.
Reduce heat to a simmer and cover. Prepare all vegetables ahead.

Remove any damaged outer leaves from the lettuces and trim the
stems and rinse well. Cut the lettuces into quarters and lower these on a
large strainer into the simmering water. Let the quarters blanch for
slightly less than a minute, then strain them out and fold each lettuce
section over into neat bundles. Gently press to remove water and set
aside.

Add the juice of 1 lemon to the simmering water.

Turn and trim the artichokes. Break off the stems and, using a
stainless-steel knife, cut off the top third. Bend back the outer leaves and
break them at their tender points (some of the lower edible portion of
each leaf will be left on the heart). Trim off the outer dark green portions
of the leaves and rub the chokes with a cut half of lemon to prevent their
discoloration. When all the chokes are turned, add them to the
simmering water and parboil for 5 minutes. Strain out the artichokes and
cut them into quarters. Lift out the interior chokes with a knife.

Peel the pearl onions and cut a small *x* in the bottom of each.
(Placing the onions in a large bowl of cool water sometimes facilitates the
peeling process.)

Cut and trim the carrots into uniform olive-shaped pieces 1½ inches long.

Snap off the stems of the snow peas and string them on both sides. Slice the zucchini into ¼-inch-thick rounds.

Clean the mushrooms with a damp, salted cloth, and cut off the stems even with the caps (use only the caps in this dish).

Trim the tender tips of the asparagus. (The peeled lengths may be added, if desired.)

Place the garlic and cream in a small, heavy saucepan. Over low heat, reduce the cream to 1 cup (stir frequently during the reduction). Strain and press the garlic cream through a sieve. Set aside.

Melt 3 tablespoons butter in a large, heatproof casserole. Add onions, carrots, *bouquet garni*, and a small ladle of stock. Allow the vegetables to simmer, uncovered, for 10 minutes. Arrange the lettuce sections on top of the onions and scatter in the artichoke quarters. Pour stock over the vegetables and cook, covered and over the lowest heat possible, for 20 minutes. Add snow peas, mushrooms, zucchini, and asparagus to the pot and salt lightly. Recover and cook for another 10 minutes. (The top vegetables should, in effect, steam and remain somewhat crisp.)

Remove vegetables from heat and draw off all possible liquid with a bulb baster. Remove *bouquet garni* and hold the vegetables in a warming oven. Place the liquid and the juice of 1 lemon in the sauté pan and reduce as rapidly as possible to about 1½ cups. Off the heat, start adding the remaining butter chunks, whisking and shaking the pan as you do so. Whisk in the reduced cream, fresh herbs, and pepper. (The initial saltiness of the stock will determine the need for seasoning; taste carefully.)

Draw off any last bit of liquid that has accumulated under the vegetables, then pour over the buttery sauce and give the pot a good shake to mix the elements. Ladle immediately into preheated bowls. Serve with goodly chunks of fresh bread.   Serves 10 to 12

GREEN SALAD AND CHEESES

THE SALAD need be only a symbolic gesture. A few rough greens with an acidic dressing will do, as fine lettuce has already appeared in the main course. Four or 5 pretty cheeses on cheese baskets or set upon platters covered with grape or fig leaves should suffice. A nice assortment would be a nutty Gruyère or Appenzeller; a Canadian or Vermont cheddar; a soft Pont-l'Eveque, Reblochon, or Brie; a goat cheese; and a blue cheese. Serve with crackers rather than bread.

MOUSSE OF PEARS WITH APRICOT SAUCE

> 1¼ pounds firm pears, plus 6 perfect pears for
>   poaching
> ¼ cup water
> ⅔ cup sugar
> 4 egg yolks
> 2 cups milk, scalded
> 1 tablespoon (envelope) unflavored gelatine,
>   softened in 2 tablespoons water
> 1 tablespoon pear brandy (Poire), optional
> ¾ cup heavy cream

Sugar syrup: 1 cup sugar
                 2 cups water
                 1 teaspoon vanilla extract

Sauce: 1 cup dried apricots
                 ½ cup water
                 1 tablespoon lemon juice

PEEL, CORE, AND SLICE 1¼ pounds of pears. Place pears and water in a saucepan and stew over low heat until the pears dissolve into a purée. Stir frequently to prevent scorching. Continue cooking and stirring until the pears appear very thick and dry. Set aside to cool.

Beat sugar and egg yolks together until thick and creamy. Slowly stir the hot milk into the eggs. Add the softened gelatine and place the mixture over medium-low heat. Stir continuously until the mixture starts to thicken. (Watch for steam rising from the surface or small bubbles forming around the edge.) Do not allow the liquid to begin to boil or the eggs will curdle. Remove from heat and stir in the pear purée and optional pear brandy. Leave to cool in the refrigerator.

Just as the pear mixture begins to feel cool, whip the cream until it is thick but not stiff (over-whipped cream dries a mousse rather than allowing it to remain moist and finely textured). Fold the cream into the pears and pour the mixture into an oiled 8-cup charlotte or soufflé mold. Cover and chill until set.

Make the sugar syrup. Combine sugar and water. Bring to a boil, then turn the heat down and simmer for 8 minutes. Add the vanilla to the syrup.

Using a stainless-steel knife, peel the 6 perfect pears, leaving them whole and with the stems intact. Place them immediately in the syrup and poach the pears until just tender. Strain out the pears and allow them to cool.

Place dried apricots, 1 cup of syrup, and water in a pan. Simmer until the apricots are tender. Press the apricots and their cooking liquid through a sieve or purée them in a food processor. Add lemon juice (and a bit of pear brandy, if desired). The apricot sauce should be of light, pouring consistency, so thin it with water if need be.

Unmold the mousse upon a rimmed platter. Place the pears around it and coat mousse and pears with the pretty sauce.   Serves 12

Praline Cake

1⅓ cups ground blanched almonds
3¼ cups sugar
⅓ cup flour
10 large eggs, separated and at room temperature
2 sticks unsalted butter
1 teaspoon vanilla extract
1¾ cups sliced almonds (skins on)
5 ounces semisweet chocolate

PREHEAT OVEN TO 350 DEGREES. Butter and flour a baking sheet. Trace 2 10-inch circles in the flour and set aside.

Combine ground almonds, 1½ cups sugar, and flour in a bowl and mix well. Fold a large sheet of heavy paper in half and place the nut mixture along the crease in the center.

Beat the egg whites by hand, preferably in a clean copper bowl, until they form stiff peaks. Slowly, evenly, fold nuts into egg whites. (If you are working by yourself, sit on a stool, hold the bowl of egg whites between your knees, lift the paper with the nuts by its ends, and slowly add the nuts with one hand while the other hand gently folds the 2 elements together with a spatula.) Do not over-mix. Divide the batter between the 2 traced circles, and smooth the mixture into even rounds with the spatula. Bake immediately for around 40 minutes. (Protect with foil from over-browning, if necessary.) Let the cakes cool for 5 minutes, then transfer the rounds to cake racks so they can dry and crisp. Trim to perfect rounds.

Prepare a praline. Place 1 cup of sugar and ½ cup of water in a small, heavy pan. Place over medium heat and, without stirring, let the mixture turn to a soft gold, then a deeper amber. Watch for a small puff of blue smoke and sniff at the mixture. When it is dark amber and the first, slightly acrid smell reaches the nose, remove the caramel from the stove and add immediately 1¼ cups of sliced almonds. Swirl the pan and turn out the contents onto an oiled baking sheet or marble counter. Let the caramelized almonds cool completely, then grind to a fine powder in food processor or blender.

In the bowl of a mixer (or with a hand mixer), beat the egg yolks with remaining sugar until they form a thick, pale sponge. Scrape the eggs into another bowl. Place the butter in the mixer and beat it until it is creamed. In 3 or 4 portions, beat the egg sponge into the butter. (If the mixture seems to curdle at all, just continue beating until the butter cream heats somewhat; it will reform a homogenous blending.) Stir the praline powder into the butter cream.

To assemble the cake, spread a thick layer of butter cream over 1 cake round and place it on a circle of heavy cardboard for easy handling. Place the other layer on top and frost smoothly with the remaining butter cream. Sprinkle the remaining ½ cup of sliced almonds over the surface. Melt the chocolate over hot water. Pipe 5 stripes of chocolate in parallel lines across top of the cake. Refrigerate for 12 to 24 hours before eating.

Serves 10 to 12

APPLE TART WITH PINE NUTS

5 to 6 tart, crisp apples (Winesaps, Cortlands,
 Yellow Delicious)
½ cup pine nuts
¾ cup sugar
1 teaspoon cinnamon
3 tablespoons butter, cut in thin shavings
½ cup red currant jelly

Pâte Sucrée: 8 tablespoons unsalted butter
2 tablespoons sugar
1 egg
½ teaspoon vanilla extract
1 teaspoon lemon juice
1½ cups all-purpose flour

TO MAKE THE CRUST, cream together the butter and sugar. Stir in the
egg, vanilla, and lemon juice. Add the flour and, working with the
fingertips, combine the ingredients into a smooth ball. Wrap the pastry in
plastic wrap and refrigerate for at least 30 minutes. (Let the pastry remain
at room temperature a few minutes before it is rolled.)

Preheat the oven to 350 degrees.

On a lightly floured surface, roll out the dough and transfer it to a
large 12 to 14-inch tart pan, preferably with a removable bottom (or you
might use 2 smaller flan rings). Patch the dough if necessary by
moistening any ragged edges and pushing them together. Cover the
dough with a sheet of aluminum foil and weight down the foil with
dried beans. Bake the crust for 10 minutes. Remove beans and foil.

Peel and core the apples and cut them into slices a good ¼ inch
thick. Arrange the slices in overlapping concentric circles. Sprinkle the
surface with pine nuts, ½ cup sugar, cinnamon, and butter shavings.
Turn up the oven heat to 375 degrees and bake the tart for 25 to 30
minutes.

Melt the red currant jelly over gentle heat. Brush the surface of the
tart with the jelly and sprinkle ¼ cup sugar over the surface. Place the
tart briefly under a preheated broiler until the sugar and jam just begin to
caramelize. Remove the ring from around the tart and transfer the tart,
still on its metal base, to a large paper doily.   Serves 10 to 12

FROZEN BITTERSWEET CHOCOLATE

12 ounces extra bittersweet chocolate (Tobler or Lindt)
4 tablespoons water
1 stick unsalted butter, cut into pieces
8 eggs, separated and at room temperature
½ cup sugar
1 teaspoon vanilla extract
1 tablespoon cognac
2 squares semisweet chocolate
Stiffly whipped cream

PREPARE A 9 BY 9-INCH BAKING PAN TO ACT AS A MOLD. Lightly oil the interior of the pan (use any vegetable oil), and cut a square of kitchen parchment or wax paper to fit the mold's bottom. Place paper in dish.

Break the chocolate into small pieces. Place chocolate and water in a double boiler and melt the chocolate over hot water. Off the heat, add the butter bit by bit until it has all melted.

Beat the egg yolks with the sugar until thick and lemon colored. Stir chocolate into the eggs. Add vanilla and cognac.

Beat the egg whites, preferably by hand in a clean copper bowl, until they are stiff but still glossy. Stir ⅓ of the whites completely into the chocolate mixture, then fold in the remaining eggs until well blended.

Pour the chocolate into the prepared mold. Cover with plastic wrap or foil and place in the freezer at least overnight.

Grate the chocolate squares on the large holes of a hand grater.

Loosen the dessert by first running a knife around the edges then dipping the bottom of the pan briefly into very hot water. Unmold onto a paper-doily–covered tray and peel away the parchment or wax paper. Smooth grated chocolate over the surface.

Pipe whipped cream from a rosette tube around the border of the square. The dessert should sit in the refrigerator to soften slightly before it is needed. Serves 10 to 12

Note: A large bowl containing 2 cups of stiffly whipped and sweetened cream should be placed among the desserts so that guests can help themselves.

Summer Productions/Taurus Photos

A
CHARCUTERIE
COCKTAIL
PARTY

The Inspiration

. . . the handsome and inviting charcuteries of France.

French food shops have always been a source of both decorative and culinary inspiration, for one never walks down streets in any town or village in France without finding breads in fascinating shapes, pâtés and terrines adorned with simple decorative designs, and pastries touched with an artisan's hand. In a small notebook I sketch the design or jot down an idea; then, returning home later, I recreate the object, experimenting and perfecting until it resembles completely the original source. In such a fashion are many recipes devised.

It was on such an excursion in Hyères, a small resort town in southern France, that I once saw a charcuterie shop window so perfect and appealing that I knew it must be recreated entirely for a party. Charcuteries traditionally sell prepared meats, particularly pork, but this shop extended the variety of its offerings, and its front window included not only galantines, *boudins* (blood puddings), and

A CHARCUTERIE COCKTAIL PARTY

endless sausages, but also a variety of salads, each containing some small amount of crumbled bacon or minced ham—just enough to justify its presence in the store. Placed at the top of the display in a field of parsley green was a marvelous bread in the shape of a pig.

The entire collection of dishes fits most easily into the framework of a cocktail party, an occasional Entertainment that is sometimes necessary but rarely well executed. Set at an awkward time that often extends into the dining hour, the traditional cocktail party too often offers wan selections of crackers and cheeses, sliced limp gray meat, stale canapés, and other generally uninspiring foods that satisfy neither soul nor appetite. It has always seemed to me that if one extends hospitality, it should not be half hearted. Particularly is an honest meal necessary for working people who arrive with healthy appetites. When cocktails are concerned, it is an unthinking host who does not provide sufficient ballast for imbibing hungry guests.

Setting the Scene

Because the food for this Entertainment must be amassed in a striking and generous display, it is necessary that it be arranged in a large, open space and in a location which will not impede the flow of people as they congregate around the area. Certainly the bar should be placed at some distance from the food.

String up, if possible, a variety of sausages above and around the area where the food is to be dispensed. Choose a slightly small table and crowd it to overflowing rather than spreading out serving dishes in a colder, more formal arrangement. (Likewise, when one offers food in a dish, the amount should fill the container, for abundance—which can easily be suggested in the manner in which food is presented—is psychologically comforting to guests.) There should be many knives about for slicing sausages and bread, and a nearby serving station might also offer silverware and plates both small and large, the latter to encourage guests who need to feed themselves more fully.

You can, if you wish, make a display loaf of fresh bread (page 142) in the shape of a pig to advertise the theme. Though for purposes of clarity there are only a few labels in the accompanying photograph, the entire charcuterie spread should be identified with small signs proclaiming the name of every salad, sausage, and cheese and, if you wish, the price of the object in francs.

You should be able to compile everything for a large party at least a day ahead, and the following menu allows you to do so. Leftover salads will keep for several days. Choose a few large cheeses like cheddars and gruyère, which can be used up later in cooking. The offering of apples, pears, and oranges allows guests who might linger to top off their meal with a bit of sweetness. If one is left with an oversupply, the fruits can be stored and turned into juice, applesauce, or desserts over a period of time.

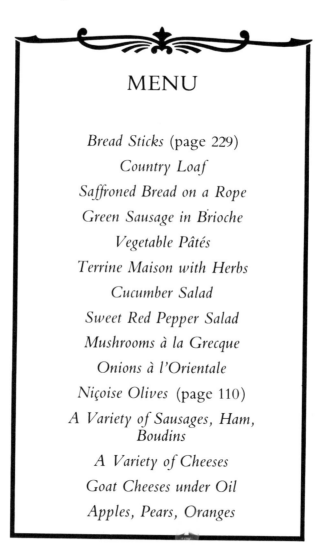

MENU

Bread Sticks (page 229)

Country Loaf

Saffroned Bread on a Rope

Green Sausage in Brioche

Vegetable Pâtés

Terrine Maison with Herbs

Cucumber Salad

Sweet Red Pepper Salad

Mushrooms à la Grecque

Onions à l'Orientale

Niçoise Olives (page 110)

A Variety of Sausages, Ham, Boudins

A Variety of Cheeses

Goat Cheeses under Oil

Apples, Pears, Oranges

Country Loaf

2 batches Fresh Bread dough (page 142)

A large, flat 14- or 15-inch basket, with 3-inch sides
1 yard linen, canvas, or duck material
5-inch bowl or can
An unpainted, metal clothes hanger, or an old knife-sharpening
   steel

TO ACT AS A MOLDING FORM FOR THE BREAD, choose a basket with a perfectly flat bottom and straight sides. I have a permanent basket for this loaf, and I sewed the material to the interior bottom and sides by stitching light kitchen string through the cloth and around the loosely woven basket frame. It is possible, however, to simply place cloth in a basket and trim the excess at the corners. Coat the cloth with an even ⅛ inch of flour. Oil a can or bowl and place it at the center of the basket. Set aside.

Mix the batches of bread in 2 separate bowls. Knead each separately for 8 minutes, then combine the batches and knead together for 3 minutes. Place the large amount of dough in a clean, oiled bowl, cover with a towel, and let rise for a good hour in a warm place or until doubled in bulk.

Punch down the dough and form it into a neat ball by tucking and stretching the surface dough under until the round retains its shape. Lift the dough ball and plunge the stiff fingers of both hands through the center from opposite directions. Place the bread basket directly beneath the dough. Quickly start pulling apart and expanding the center hole while the dough mass rolls over and over the tops of the hands (see photograph 1). When the dough has opened into an even circle, place it down and around the can in the center of the basket (see photograph 2). Press and manipulate the dough into an even circle. Cover with a towel and leave to rise until the dough reaches the top of the basket.

Oil a 15-inch pizza pan or a large baking sheet. Place the sheet on top of the basket. Holding the pan and basket together, flip the two over, then lift off the basket and gently pull out the center can (photograph 3). Do any necessary tucking to neaten the circle, and enlarge the center hole slightly.

With a sharp knife, cut slits half way into the dough until the form has been neatly divided into 8 portions (see photograph 4). Tuck in and round the outer points of the 8 portions so that they resemble flower petals. With the same sharp knife, cut a quick circle ¼ inch deep around the middle top of the dough. Let the bread rise for another 20 minutes so that it can recover the volume it lost when it was so rudely forced from the basket. Preheat oven to 400 degrees.

Place bread in oven and let bake for 20 minutes. Lower the temperature to 350 degrees and bake for another 30 minutes. Turn off the oven; the bread should be done in 15 minutes. (Test the loaf by giving the bottom a knock with your knuckles; it should feel and sound dry and hollow.) Cool the bread on a cake rack or slightly prop the loaf so escaping steam does not soften the undercrust.

To emblazon a toasted pattern on the loaf, untwist the coat hanger and straighten the metal. Bend the metal into thirds and twist the lengths together as much as possible so that they form a somewhat solid length. Holding one end in a hand protected with an oven mit, heat the other end of the metal in a flame or directly on a burner. When the metal is very hot, scorch lines at each of the 8 indentions and around the circle in the center (photograph 5). Reheat metal as needed. Let bread cool at least half a day before serving.   Serves 20 to 24

Saffroned Bread on a Rope

1½ envelopes dry yeast
1 teaspoon sugar
½ teaspoon powdered saffron
2¼ cups warm water
1 egg, well beaten
2 teaspoons salt
¼ cup freshly grated Parmesan cheese
6 to 6½ cups unbleached flour
1 egg yolk
1 tablespoon water
Whole saffron pistils

1 yard thick, hempen rope

DISSOLVE YEAST, sugar, and all but a large pinch of the powdered saffron in warm water. Add egg, salt, and cheese, and stir until smooth. Add flour until the dough forms a mass that can be turned out onto a counter. Knead and continue adding flour until the dough feels elastic and no longer sticky. Work the dough well, then place in an oiled bowl, cover with a towel, and leave to rise for a good hour or until doubled in bulk.

1

2

5

Punch down and form the dough into a ball. Gently stretch and pull the surface dough and tuck it under the ball 2 or 3 times to help the mass keep its tensile shape. Lift the dough ball and plunge the stiff fingers of both hands through the center from opposite directions. Roll the dough over and over in your hands until the center opens and you have a large, well-shaped donut. Place the dough on an oiled baking sheet.

Beat the egg yolk with water and the reserved large pinch of saffron. Brush the glaze over the bread, and sprinkle the surface with whole saffron pistils. Let the bread rise for 30 to 40 minutes in a warm place. Preheat the oven to 350 degrees.

Put bread to bake in oven for around 1 hour. Remove and let the loaf cool briefly on a cake rack. Tie the rope through the center hole for a rustic, decorative effect.   Serves 8 to 10 people

Note that the amount of dough given in the following brioche recipe is enough for both this Green Sausage and the following Vegetable Pâté.

3   4

GREEN SAUSAGE IN BRIOCHE

Sausage:
5 ounces spinach, washed and stemmed
4 slices firm bread, crusts removed
1 medium onion, chopped fine
3 tablespoons unsalted butter
8 chicken livers, chopped
1 tablespoon cognac, heated
2 large cloves garlic, pressed
2 pounds boneless, skinless chicken breasts and
    thighs, ground
1 teaspoon finely crumbled mixed herbs (thyme,
    oregano, savory)
1 teaspoon salt
Freshly ground pepper
A few grains of cayenne
1 medium egg

Brioche:
1½ envelopes dry yeast
6 tablespoons warm milk
3 cups flour, preferably unbleached
1 teaspoon salt
3 large eggs at room temperature
7 tablespoons unsalted butter, softened
1 egg yolk beaten with 2 tablespoons water

Aluminum foil

COOK THE SPINACH in only the water clinging to its leaves until it turns bright green. Refresh under a spray of cool water, then squeeze the leaves as dry as possible and blot them with toweling. Chop finely.

Soak the bread briefly in water, then squeeze it dry and crumble it.

Cook the onion in butter until it softens. Strain out the onion and, in the butter remaining in the pan, sauté the chicken livers over brisk heat, stirring constantly until they turn pale but retain a slight pinkness at the interior. Immediately add the cognac and light a match to the frying pan. When the flames have subsided, press down on the livers to extract all their juices, then strain them from the pan. Reduce the remaining liquid to 1 tablespoon.

Combine reduced liquid, spinach, bread, livers, and all the remaining ingredients for the sausages and mix well. For the best consistency, purée the mixture in a food processor.

Tear off 4 sheets of aluminum foil, each 12 inches in length. Butter or oil one side of the foil. Divide the sausage mixture into 4 portions and spoon out a portion along the long buttered edge of each piece of foil. Roll up the foil and twist the ends together to provide a sausage casing. Preheat the oven to 350 degrees.

Place a roasting pan containing 1½ inches of hot water in oven. Place in the sausages and let them poach for 45 minutes. Remove 1 of the sausages and open it. If the sausage does not feel completely firm, let it cook another 10 minutes. Drain all poaching liquid from the sausages.

Let sausages cool in their foil casings, then refrigerate until needed. These may be made a day or two ahead. Yields 4 sausages

To prepare the brioche, dissolve the yeast in the milk. Place flour and salt in a large bowl and make a well in the center. Break in the eggs, add the yeast, then work the ingredients into a smooth dough. (A mixer with a flat blade makes short, 5-minute work of this sticky process.) There should be a distinct elasticity to the developed dough.

Add the butter and continue mixing for another 3 minutes. Scrape the dough into a clean, oiled bowl. Cover with a towel, and let rise for 1 hour in a warm location. Chill the dough for 30 minutes before forming sausages.

Oil a large baking sheet.

To form the sausages, unwrap each chicken-liver sausage, brush it lightly with egg yolk and water, then roll the sausage in flour. This coating will allow the brioche dough to adhere to its surface.

Press and stretch the dough out on the baking sheet and enfold the sausages. You can make 4 short sausages or 2 long lengths; or it is possible to use 2 sausages and form a horseshoe shape (see photograph, page 191). Place seam-side down on baking tray. Form leftover scraps into decorations. Brush the dough with the remaining egg yolk and water to form a glaze. Let rise 30 to 45 minutes. Preheat the oven to 375 degrees.

Bake in oven for 40 minutes or until the crust is nicely browned.

Serves at least 20

Vegetable Pâtés

1½ pounds veal, weighed after boning and trimming
1 egg plus 2 egg whites
Finely grated zest of 1 lemon
1 pound tender green beans
1 pound carrots, scraped
1 pound turnips, peeled
1 pound asparagus
1 cup heavy cream
6 tablespoons unsalted butter, melted and cooled
1 teaspoon minced parsley
1 teaspoon salt
Freshly ground pepper, nutmeg

Brioche Dough (the dough from the preceding recipe is
    sufficient for both Green Sausage in Brioche and Vegetable
    Pâtés)

CUT THE VEAL INTO SMALL CUBES. Put veal, egg and whites, and
lemon zest in the bowl of a food processor, and process until purée-
smooth. Scrape the purée into a small bowl and press a piece of plastic
wrap directly down on top of the meat so no crust can form over the
surface. Refrigerate for 1 hour while preparing the rest of the ingredients.

Stem, string, and rinse the beans. Cut them into small dice. (All the
vegetables will profit from being cut by hand but, in a pinch, a machine
can do the job, though the results will not be impeccable.)

Slice the carrots thinly and cut them into dice. Cut the turnips into
dice. Slice the tender portions of the asparagus into rounds and then chop
them into rough dice.

Bring a large pot of well-salted water to the boil. Add beans,
carrots, and turnips. Simmer for 2 minutes, then add the asparagus and
continue cooking for another minute. Strain out the vegetables and
immediately run a spray of cold water over them for 1 minute to set the
color and stop the cooking process. The vegetables should remain
slightly crisp. Drain well, then refrigerate until completely chilled.
Continue to drain off any liquid as it accumulates, and blot the vegetables
with paper toweling to ensure their dryness.

Generously butter 2 standard oblong bread tins and set aside.

Place a pan large enough to hold the 2 molds in the oven and add 1
inch of water. Preheat oven to 350 degrees.

Fifteen minutes before the pâtés are to be assembled, place the cream in the freezer along with a large mixing bowl. The brioche dough should also be slightly chilled.

Whip the cream until it is thick but not stiff.

Place the puréed meat in the bowl of the food processor and begin to purée it. Slowly pour in the melted butter and continue mixing until it is smoothly incorporated. Scrape the meat into the chilled mixing bowl and work in half the cream. Add chilled vegetables, parsley, salt, pepper, and 5 scrapings of nutmeg. Fold in the remaining cream and divide the pâté mixture into the 2 buttered molds.

Immediately roll out the brioche dough and pat it into place directly on top of the vegetable mixture. Cut a hole in the center of the dough for escaping steam, and rapidly use the scrapes to form a simple, decorative design.

Place the pâtés in the *bain-marie* in the oven and bake for 45 minutes or until the brioche covering is a handsome brown and a skewer, inserted into the steam hole, comes out clean.

Let the molds cool to room temperature in the pan of water, then chill at least 8 hours before unmolding. To unmold, run a knife around the pâtés and gently slip them out of the molds and onto their sides, then right them on a serving platter.   Serves at least 16

GOAT CHEESES UNDER OIL

Several goat banons, *or* Montrachet cheeses, *or* scoops of firm
    feta cheese
Olive oil
Peppercorns (black, white, pink, if available)
Bay leaves
Fresh sprigs of herbs (thyme, oregano, rosemary, savory)
3 to 4 cloves garlic, peeled
Freshly ground black pepper

THIS IS A PROVENÇAL WAY of serving very fresh, small cheeses, but it can be used effectively with more ripened cheeses also. Simply cover the cheeses with oil, add several peppercorns, herbs, and garlic cloves, and refrigerate for around 6 hours before serving. A serving consists of a cheese with 1 or 2 tablespoons of oil as a dressing. Grind black pepper over the cheese and accompany with good bread.

Terrine Maison with Herbs

> 2 pounds calves liver
> 6 ounces salt pork, well chilled
> 2 medium-large onions, coarsely chopped
> 3 cloves garlic, minced
> 5 slices firm white bread, crusts removed
> 1 teaspoon salt
> Freshly ground black pepper
> 4 large eggs
> 4 tablespoons unsalted butter, softened
> 2 tablespoons minced parsley
> 1 teaspoon mixed dried herbs (thyme, oregano,
>   savory, pulverized rosemary)
> ½ pound thinly sliced fatback
> 1 cup chicken stock
> 1 tablespoon cognac

To coat the   Melted butter
terrine: Mixed dried herbs

REMOVE ANY FATTY TISSUE or veins from the calves liver and cut it into 1-inch cubes.

Rinse all salt from the salt pork. Cut into dice by slicing down to the rind then cutting the fat across into small cubes.

Combine liver, salt pork, onions, and garlic and grind through the medium blade of a meat grinder or process very briefly in a food processor.

Soak the bread briefly in water, then wring the mass dry and finely crumble the bread. Using your hands, mix meat, bread, salt, generous pepper, eggs, butter, and herbs to a finely homogenized mixture. Preheat the oven to 350 degrees.

Butter or oil a terrine or soufflé dish (I use a rustic, handled *pöelon*). Line the bottom and sides of the dish with thin strips of fat, then pack in the meat mixture. Place a few strips of fat across the top, and cover loosely with foil.

Bake in oven for 1 hour and 15 minutes. Heat chicken stock and cognac. Three or four times during the baking period, pour warm, moistening stock over the terrine until it is used up.

Remove foil and the remains of the top barding fat. Melt butter and pour over the surface of the terrine until the meat is entirely covered. Let the terrine cool to room temperature, then refrigerate. When the fat has hardened, smooth a decorative coating of mixed dried herbs over the surface. This terrine is now fully protected, and it will keep for up to a week in the refrigerator. Let season at least 24 hours before serving.

Serves 12 to 15

CUCUMBER SALAD

3 to 4 long cucumbers, preferably burpless, well scrubbed
Salt
3 cloves garlic, peeled and crushed
2 bay leaves
10 peppercorns
10 coriander seeds
Sprigs of fresh thyme, *or* 1 teaspoon dried thyme
2 cloves
2 cups white wine vinegar
2 cups water
3- or 4-ounce bottle pickled onions, drained
Olive oil
6 slices of bacon, fried and crumbled (optional)

CUT THE CUCUMBERS into 1-inch-thick slices or, for a more decorative effect, cut the slices into zigzag lion's tooth patterns with slanted cuts of a small sharp knife. Place cucumbers in a large bowl and sprinkle generously with salt. Let the cucumbers sit for 1 hour and disgorge their water.

Prepare a cooking broth. Place garlic, herbs and spices, vinegar, and water in a stainless-steel pot and simmer for 10 minutes. Reheat immediately before the cucumbers are to cook.

Drain the cucumbers very well and plunge them into the simmering broth. Cover and bring to a boil, then reduce the heat and simmer for 10 minutes. Gently lift and stir the cucumbers from time to time. Turn off the heat and let the vegetables cool in the juices. Strain out and refrigerate at least overnight.

To assemble the salad, combine cucumbers and pickled onions. Coat lightly with olive oil, and place in a serving dish. If you wish, just before serving, fry bacon and crumble it over the top of the dish for textural interest.

Serves 15

Sweet Red Pepper Salad

6 to 8 large sweet red peppers
Salt, pepper
2 teaspoons fresh thyme leaves *or* chopped parsley and chives
1 tablespoon red wine vinegar
½ cup olive oil
Oil-cured olives (French or Greek)

PEEL THE PEPPERS by placing them over the coals of a dying fire on an oiled grill, or under a hot broiler. Turn the peppers continuously until they blister and darken on all sides as well as the top and bottom. Lift and move the peppers carefully with 2 wooden spoons. Do not pierce them with a fork at any point.

When the peppers have thoroughly scorched, remove them to a platter and cover with foil. Let them cool until they can be easily handled.

Place a large sieve over a bowl. Peel the peppers over the sieve so that any dripping juices (which will form an integral part of the salad's dressing) can be saved. Peel the peppers, then open them and pull out all seeds. Cut the pepper flesh into ½-inch strips.

Press down on all the matter within the sieve so that every bit of savory juice is expressed. Discard the debris. Add salt, pepper, thyme, and vinegar to the juices. Add olive oil: Beat well with a fork, then taste for seasoning. Add more salt or vinegar as necessary. (There should be a good cup of dressing.)

Place the peppers in a serving dish, pour over the sauce, and refrigerate for a day before serving. Garnish with a handful of olives, and serve just slightly cool.   Serves 10 to 12

Mushrooms à la Greque

1½ cups water
½ cup dry white wine
½ cup olive oil
¼ teaspoon salt
15 coriander seeds
15 white peppercorns
2 bay leaves
1 large *bouquet garni* (parsley, thyme, celery)
1 pound large, fresh mushrooms

Garnish: Minced parsley
3 lemons

PLACE WATER, wine, oil, salt, spices, bay leaves, and *bouquet garni* in a non-aluminum pot and boil for 5 minutes.

Trim off any tough portions of bottom stems from the mushrooms, and wipe them with a damp cloth. (If they are very dirty, rinse them under water.) Put the mushrooms in the liquid and simmer for around 5 minutes. Test one of the mushrooms and allow them to remain slightly firm. Strain out the mushrooms, and return the liquid to a boil. Reduce over a strong flame by about half.

Place the mushrooms in a gratin dish. Remove the *bouquet garni* but leave the seeds and bay leaves. Pour the reduced liquid over the mushrooms and leave to cool to room temperature. Cover and refrigerate the mushrooms overnight.

Refrigeration tends to negate seasoning somewhat, so be sure to taste the mushroom liquid before serving. Add salt or lemon juice if more acidity is required. Garnish the mushrooms with a sprinkle of minced parsley, and place a rim of thinly cut lemon slices around the edge of the dish. Serve cool but not exceedingly chilled.   Serves 12

ONIONS À L'ORIENTALE

⅓ cup raisins
2 pounds pearl onions
1 large white or yellow onion, finely chopped
2 cloves garlic, minced
½ cup olive oil
4 very large tomatoes, peeled, seeded, and chopped, *or* a 28-
    ounce can Italian tomatoes, drained and chopped
Scant ¼ teaspoon powdered saffron
½ teaspoon salt
Freshly ground pepper
Cayenne to taste
1 tablespoon brown sugar
¾ cup white wine
Juice of 2 large lemons
Minced parsley

PLACE THE RAISINS IN A SMALL PAN, cover with water, and bring to a boil. Remove from the heat and let the raisins plump for 15 minutes. Drain.

Peel the onions. This thankless task is best performed by placing the onions in a large bowl of cold water for 10 minutes before and during peeling. Use a stainless-steel knife and score a small *x* in the stem end of each onion to help it retain its shape during cooking.

Cook the large, chopped onion and the garlic in oil over low heat. When the onion is tender, add tomatoes, spices, seasonings, sugar, and raisins. Stew over gentle heat for 10 minutes, stirring frequently. Add the peeled onions, the white wine, and the lemon juice. Cover the pan and simmer for 25 minutes or until the onions are just tender but before they have a chance to begin disintegrating.

Strain the onions through a colander or sieve and return only the juices to the pan. Reduce juices to half their volume, then add the strained onions and the raisins. Continue simmering, uncovered, until the mixture is very thickly coated with rich tomato sauce.

Place onions in a pretty gratin or quiche dish, sprinkle the top with minced parsley, and let the salad cool. Serve at room temperature or just slightly chilled. Serves 12

THE DIM SUM PARLOR

The Inspiration

. . . the delightful Chinese custom of taking yum cha, *the Cantonese expression which means to sip tea.*

"Let's go *yum cha*," says a Chinese host, and he means not only to treat you to a warming dish of fragrant tea, but also to offer an enticing array of dim sum, or tea-time snacks. There are restaurants that specialize in dim sum, and from early in the morning to around 4 in the afternoon, people drop in for refreshments or a light meal, or to simply while away time with a newspaper and a cup of tea. Continuously as you sit at table, a procession of waiters pushing carts winds among the customers like an animated cafeteria. Each cart contains a different offering, and you have only to choose and point to receive a portion of whatever is passing. (There is nothing quite like the experience in Western cuisine. The closest one comes is the menu of degustation offered in certain *nouvelle cuisine* restaurants, where one receives an ordered variety of eight or ten dishes, all specialties of the house, in very

THE DIM
SUM
PARLOR

small quantities. In effect, one eats a string of appetizers and first courses and never comes to the large main portion of heavy meat that usually stabilizes a meal, though that meaty dish is also offered in three or four bites. The degustation experience always strikes me, by the way, as a feminine rather than a masculine occasion.)

In the dim sum parlor then one eats, with a certain naughty pleasure, only those crisp-fried tidbits, those delectable morsels that are usually appetizers. Carts roll by with Pork Ribs in Black Bean Sauce; Fried Shrimp Balls; Golden Pork Dumplings; Rice Stick with Shrimp; Chicken Bundles. Sweets like Coconut Jello and Lotus Seed Delight alternate with savories. A strange lavender substance passes (pig's blood reduced with broth to a solid, then steamed and moistened with more broth). No, thank you? Then try a dish of two Baked Roast Pork Buns, plump as a baby's bottom . . . you can sit all afternoon if you wish.

When the meal is finished, the customer motions to the waiter. The shape of each empty dish on the table signals its price. Whatever was in the large round bowls cost $2.00 each; the small oval dishes are $1.20. The waiter makes a rapid mental calculation and presents the surprisingly inexpensive bill. Then he clears the dishes, whips off the table's covering oilcloth (the cloths are stacked twenty deep), and more waiting customers slip into the seats to *yum cha*.

Setting the Scene

The dim sum pattern of entertaining can be useful for many occasions. It might provide a light, after-theater meal or, minus the dessert, an unusual cocktail party. Because most of its dishes are composed ahead of time, it can also prove to be one of those few occasions when the cook can truly be a guest at his or her own party, for a hired teenager could easily act as waiter.

Have all serving portions prepared in advance and covered tightly with plastic wrap. Spring rolls can be kept in a warming oven, and only the dumplings need to be given their final six-minute frying. Have chopsticks for everyone. Place the bowls of dipping sauce in the center of the table, if possible on a lazy Susan. (Inexpensive lazy Susan wheels found at most hardware stores can be topped with a large round of plywood and then a pretty serving tray, and thus you can authentically serve guests at all sides of the table.) The melon dessert, set in a bowl of cracked ice, is also effectively presented on a revolving base.

Serve portions on a large brass tray or wheel them by on a cart. Have a large pot of fragrant green tea close by the table or let a waiter pour it frequently. Do, of course, make the dining area as exotic as possible (see page 299). I delight in having a piece of vinyl or oilcloth for a table covering because it allows a small dramatic moment toward the end of the meal. Just before dessert, when all plates have been cleared, amuse the guests by cleaning the table in true dim-sum style. Spill a small stream of hot tea onto the oilcloth from the teapot, then quickly wipe up all crumbs. How very sensible.

THE
MENU
(FOR 10 TO 12)

Shrimp and Black Mushrooms

*Spring Rolls with Glutinous
Rice*

*Rice Noodles with Almonds
and Hot Pepper Sauce*

Golden Pan-fried Dumplings

Pine Nut Cones

Fruits in Ginger Syrup

SHRIMP AND BLACK MUSHROOMS

30 large dried black mushrooms (Shiitake)
2 tablespoons soy sauce
1 pound shelled, deveined shrimp, plus 30 large
    shrimps in the shells
¼ cup diced salt pork
4 water chestnuts, fresh if possible, peeled and
    minced
1 egg white
1 tablespoon white wine vinegar
1 teaspoon sesame oil
1 teaspoon salt
Black pepper
Large pinch of freshly grated gingerroot
Cornstarch

Sauce:

1 teaspoon cornstarch
4 tablespoons sugar
3 tablespoons white wine vinegar
½ teaspoon salt
2 tablespoons peanut oil
⅓ cup minced scallions
2 cloves garlic, minced
2 teaspoons sesame oil
Black and white sesame seeds
Chinese or plain parsley

COVER THE MUSHROOMS IN COOL WATER and soak them for 30 minutes. Drain the mushrooms and press them to remove water. Reserve ⅓ cup of soaking liquid. Cut off the mushroom stems with a sharp knife and discard. Sprinkle the gill side of the mushrooms with soy sauce.

Rinse the shelled shrimp and drain them well. Mince the shrimp, salt pork, and water chestnuts together. (Use a cleaver, or place the ingredients in a food processor and blend until smooth.) Stir in egg white, vinegar, sesame oil, salt, some good grindings of pepper, gingerroot, and 1 tablespoon of cornstarch. Mix well.

Peel and devein the large shrimp, but leave the small tail portions unpeeled.

Squeeze out the soy sauce from the mushrooms and add it to the reserved mushroom soaking liquid. Place some cornstarch in a saucer and lightly coat the gilled side of each mushroom. Spread the shrimp paste over the starched mushrooms, and smooth the paste down evenly with dampened fingers. Curl and press a peeled shrimp on top of each mushroom.

Place the mushrooms in a steamer and steam for 8 minutes. Place portions on plates.

To prepare the sauce, dilute cornstarch in 1 tablespoon of mushroom soaking liquid. Combine mushroom liquid, cornstarch, sugar, vinegar, and salt.

Heat peanut oil in a small pan. Sauté scallions and garlic for 1 minute, stirring all the while. Add the mushroom liquid and stir over high heat for 30 seconds. Remove from heat and add sesame oil.

Place some sauce over and around each mushroom portion. Sprinkle with sesame seeds and place a small sprig of parsley at the center of each shrimp. Serve warm, lukewarm or cool.

10 servings of 3 mushrooms,
or 15 servings of 2 mushrooms

SPRING ROLLS WITH GLUTINOUS RICE

1 egg
2 cups peanut or corn oil for frying
20 spring roll wrappers (choose a Shanghai-style wrapper such as the Ho-Tai brand usually found in the freezer section of specialty stores)
½ cup Dijon-style mustard
Soy sauce

Filling:

1½ cups glutinous rice
1 ounce dried black mushrooms (Shiitake)
½ pound boneless loin of pork
3 tablespoons soy sauce
1 teaspoon sugar
1 tablespoon cornstarch
2 tablespoons peanut oil
⅓ cup sliced scallions
1 tablespoon rice wine
¼ cup diced dried shrimp
½ teaspoon salt
1 teaspoon monosodium glutamate (MSG), optional
Black pepper

PLACE THE RICE IN A SIEVE or colander and rinse well under cool water. Cover rice with water and let soak for 1 hour. Drain well. Bring 2 cups of water to a boil, add the rice, and continue boiling for 4 minutes. Turn heat down and simmer for another 6 minutes. Remove from heat and lightly stir with a fork to separate the grains. Set aside.

Soak the mushrooms in cool water for 30 minutes. Cut off and discard the stems. Press the mushrooms to rid them of excessive liquid, then cut them into dice.

Cut the pork loin into thin shreds. (The easiest way is first to stiffen the meat by half-freezing it for 30 minutes.) Cut the shreds into dice. Mix the meat with 1 tablespoon of soy sauce and the sugar and cornstarch.

Heat 2 tablespoons of oil in a wok or sauté pan. When very hot, add the scallions and almost immediately, just as they have wilted, strain them out. Add the meat and stir-fry over high heat until it has uniformly changed color. Add mushrooms, rice wine, and dried shrimp, and stir-fry for 1 more minute. Remove from pan. Add 2 tablespoons soy sauce, salt, MSG, and pepper to cooked ingredients. Stir rice into meat and mix well. Let the mixture cool.

In a cup, beat the egg with a few drops of water.

To form the spring rolls, place a wrapper on the diagonal before you. (Keep all remaining wrappers stacked under plastic wrap and covered with a damp towel.) Place a generous 2 tablespoons of filling in an oval in the center. Brush egg around the edge of the wrapper. Bring the lower point up and over the filling. Fold in the 2 side points so that they overlap (the wrapper will now look somewhat like the back of an envelope). Smooth the filling down and along the bottom of the envelope if necessary, then roll up the wrapper toward its top point. Place the spring roll, with the point folded underneath, under a large sheet of plastic wrap. Continue making rolls until all are finished. (These can be rolled in the morning, covered well, refrigerated, then fried closer to dinner time if need be.)

Heat frying oil to 350 degrees in a deep-sided sauté pan or electric skillet. In 3 batches, fry the rolls for 6 minutes or until crisp and golden. Drain well on absorbent paper. Serve hot, with a sauce of Dijon mustard that has been diluted with soy sauce until it is of a light, dipping consistency. Yields 20 rolls

Rice Noodles with Almonds and Hot Pepper Sauce

2⅔ cups all-purpose flour
⅔ cup rice flour
1½ teaspoons salt
½ cup minus 1 tablespoon peanut oil
4 cups cold water
1 cup minced boiled ham
⅔ cup minced scallions
Soy sauce
Sesame oil
1½ cups blanched almonds, chopped
3 tablespoons oil for frying

Sauce:
4 tablespoons blanched almonds
1 clove garlic
1 teaspoon sugar
4 tablespoons soy sauce
2 tablespoons wine vinegar
4 tablespoons peanut oil
1 tablespoon sesame oil
1 teaspoon cayenne
Salt
¼ cup finely chopped scallions
Chinese chives or scallion greens, parboiled

MIX ALL-PURPOSE FLOUR, rice flour, and salt in a bowl. Make a well in the middle and gradually add oil and cold water, whisking the dry ingredients all the while into the liquid until the batter is smooth.

Lightly oil baking tins. (Use 8- or 9-inch round or square cake tins if you have a steamer, or use a larger 8 by 12-inch pan floating in a larger *bain-marie.* Make sure the pans are smooth and undented.) Ladle in batter, around ⅓ cup for the small pans, a generous ⅔ cup for the larger pan. The batter should be a thin layer around ⅛ inch thick. Steam for 6 minutes or, for the larger noodles, bake in a 350-degree oven until solid (around 8 minutes). Remove noodles to oiled plates (cut large ones into 6 squares first). Wipe the pans clean, and continue cooking until all noodles are finished.

Down the center of each noodle, place a mixture of chopped ham and scallions. Sprinkle lightly with soy sauce and a few drops of sesame oil. Fold the noodles over into thirds and place them, 2 to a serving and seam-side down, on plates.

Fry the chopped almonds in oil until golden brown.

To prepare the sauce, place almonds and garlic in a mortar and crush until they become a fine paste. Add sugar, soy sauce, vinegar, oils, and cayenne. Taste for seasoning and add salt if necessary.

Spoon sauce over noodles and sprinkle with scallions and fried almonds. Tie the parboiled chives around the center of each noodle. Cover dishes with plastic wrap and refrigerate until needed. Serve cool but not chilled. *Makes 10 to 12 portions*

GOLDEN PAN-FRIED DUMPLINGS

5 tablespoons peanut oil
Soy sauce
Rice wine vinegar or Chinese black vinegar
½ cup thinly sliced scallions
2 cloves garlic, sliced thin

Filling: ¾ pound ground pork (Boston butt), *or* ground
                 breast of chicken
½ cup minced scallions
2 cloves garlic, minced
1 teaspoon minced fresh gingerroot
2 tablespoons soy sauce
2 tablespoons sesame oil
¼ teaspoon black pepper

Skins: 2½ cups all-purpose flour
1 cup boiling water

MIX ALL THE INGREDIENTS FOR THE FILLING. Cover and allow to marinate in the refrigerator while preparing the dumpling skins.

Place the flour in a large mixing bowl. Gradually sprinkle the water over the flour, stirring the flour with a fork all the while. When all the water is added, gather the dough together and knead it for 5 minutes. The dough should feel firm and smooth. Roll the dough in additional flour, then cover it tightly with plastic wrap and allow it to rest for 20 minutes.

On a lightly floured surface, knead the dough again until very smooth. Divide the dough in half and, working with one half (keep the other piece tightly covered), roll out a long, even cylinder that is 1 inch thick. Divide into 20 portions. Flatten a portion with the palm of your hand then, using a rolling pin, roll out a 2½-inch oblong. Stack each skin under a towel as it is finished.

When all the dough is used, place a spoon of the meat filling at the center of each pastry. Dampen a finger slightly with water and brush it around the edges of the pastry. Fold the pastry up over the meat and pleat and pinch the edges of the dough together. (The dumplings could be frozen at this point or refrigerated on a lightly oiled dish for up to 5 hours.)

To cook the dumplings, heat 2 10-inch frying pans until very hot. Add 1½ tablespoons oil to each pan and arrange 20 dumplings in a circular pattern in both dishes. Fry over medium heat for about 2 minutes or until the dumplings are golden on the bottom. Add ⅔ cup of water to each pan. Cover pans and cook over medium heat until the water has evaporated (around 20 minutes).

Uncover and add 1 tablespoon oil to each pan. Fry another 2 minutes or until a deep, golden brown. Invert each pan over a platter and the dumplings should fall out in pattern.

Serve hot, with bowls of soy sauce and vinegar for dipping. Add half the sliced scallions and garlic to each sauce.   Yields 40 dumplings

Note: It is possible to use canned sweet red-bean paste for this dessert, but its slightly tinny taste can be avoided if one has time to make the paste at home.

PINE NUT CONES

2 cups dried Chinese red beans
1 cup pitted dates
⅔ cup ground blanched almonds
Honey
Pine nuts
Sprigs of pine needles

RINSE THE BEANS and cover them with cool water. Soak overnight.
Drain beans and cover with 1½ pints of lightly salted cold water. Bring
to a boil, then turn down the heat and simmer for 1½ hours or until the
beans are purée soft. Drain well.

Purée the beans in a food processor, or press them through a large
sieve. Place the purée in a clean, old kitchen towel. Gather the loose ends
of the towel, place the mass in the sink, and press down on the paste
with a potato masher or tamp to remove as much liquid as possible.

Purée the dates in blender or food processor. Combine dates, beans,
and almonds. Using the hands, knead in honey bit by bit until the

mixture is rich and pleasantly sweet, but with a consistency that is firm enough to be mounded and packed.

On small salad plates or cocottes, mold a portion of the paste into a cone shape. Push pine nuts symmetrically into the paste (the narrow end of the nut should be pointed into the cone). Brush the pine nuts with honey and place each dish briefly under a very hot broiler so that the nuts can rapidly turn a glazed golden color. Garnish with sprigs of pine needles. Serve at room temperature.   Yields 12 cones

FRUITS IN GINGER SYRUP

1 cup sugar
2 teaspoons powdered ginger or freshly grated gingerroot
Juice of 1 lemon
2 cups water
2 tablespoons light rum, or to taste
1 large melon to serve as container (Cranshaw or Watermelon)
Cantaloupe
Honeydew melon
Green and purple grapes
Pineapple
Strawberries

MAKE A SIMPLE LIGHT SYRUP by combining sugar, ginger, and lemon juice with water. Bring to a boil, then turn down heat and simmer for 5 minutes. Chill, then add rum.

Over a large bowl which can capture juices, hollow out the melon container by first making melon balls, then trimming out any remains of flesh. Make cantaloupe and honeydew balls. Wash and dry the grapes. Cut a thick peel from the pineapple and section the fruit into bite-sized pieces. Add a cup of juices from the fruits to the syrup (squeeze peelings if necessary). Place all fruits but strawberries in a large bowl and pour over the syrup. Let macerate for up to 5 hours, and gently turn the fruits a few times during this period. If you wish, drain off the liquid 30 minutes before serving, and place the fruit in the freezer.

Mix strawberries with the fruit and spoon the fruit into the melon container. Stick long bamboo skewers, 1 per guest, into the fruit. Each person then spears his own fruits from the common serving source.

An Evening in Naples

The Inspiration

. . . the teeming, vital streets of Naples.

Approach this lively Italian city from the sea and it appears placid enough, stretched out in a welcoming half circle along the lengthy arc of its bay. But land on the shore and all appearances of tranquility rapidly disappear. From the crowded harbor packed with boats, you climb upward toward the fortress of Sant' Elmo and all along the way, particularly in the narrow, gray lava streets of old Naples, the senses are assaulted with color, sound, and odor and the body jostled by the crowds. Women shrill at children, children howl, hawkers hawk their wares. Every other shop seems to be a *pizzerie* fragrant with the smell of herbs and oil, tomatoes and toasted cheese; or a seafood stand offering oysters or fried shrimp. Criss-crossing it all, back and forth above the streets all banner bright in the sunshine, are innumerable strands of laundry hung out to dry.

The noise, the spirit, the theatrics of the Neapolitans all seemed to translate

poli, People on the Street.
nny Jacques/Photo Researchers

219

AN
EVENING
IN NAPLES

themselves into my kitchen one night
when a dinner party that was supposed to
have been an adult affair suddenly lost its
mature moorings. A guest whose baby-
sitter failed to arrive appeared with
children in tow, and I rapidly learned that
there was no way humanly possible to
maintain the discipline of the evening. If
children come to dinner—and sometimes
this is a necessary, even desirable event—
then the evening must and will descend to
their level. Babies crawl about in the
general vicinity of their mothers; younger
children at play constantly run back into
the kitchen to touch bases with parents;
fathers are beseiged and unable to carry on
their manly conversations. The Evening in
Naples Entertainment is designed,
therefore, to speak to the situation in the
most reasonable way by incorporating
those inevitable elements of noise and
distraction with an "if you can't beat
them, join them" attitude. Let the children
howl (indeed, give them little pinches if
they don't). Noise is positively necessary
to the evening's production.

Setting the Scene

With its ease and informality, this Entertainment becomes a familial, participatory occasion. As the pattern of the meal is do-it-yourself, the effect is almost as if it were an Italian Curry Party, with the pasta providing the central dish around which are an abundance of garnishes and two simple sauces from which to choose. All the elements—bread, sauces, garnishes, "pizza"—can be prepared ahead of time so that there is only the general overseeing of the pasta and the final, at-table preparation of the Zabaglione to be executed.

In one corner of the kitchen, set up a pasta machine securely clamped to a sturdy table. Let men and older children direct the kneading and cutting process. Counterspace and rolling pins might be set aside for children to work at muddling small lumps of dough. (Make up batches of dough beforehand, with enough extra so that some can be spared.) At the other end of the kitchen, open a folding wooden laundry dryer or place two chairs back to back and separated so that a broom handle can hang between them and serve as a rack on which the pasta can dry.

Near the stove should be a counter or table on which can be grouped the assorted garnishes for the main course.

Over the dining area, criss-cross lengths of clothesline and hang a colorful assortment of laundry: towels, pillowslips, lingerie, all dry of course. Here and there about the room might appear bright geraniums and, in season, pots of basil.

To add to the general confusion underfoot, have a basket of toys with which young children can play.

On the table, spread a red-and-white checkered cloth. Give everyone a large Bordeaux wine glass and fan a red checkered napkin in its bowl. For a centerpiece, place a basket containing breadsticks and that good old collegiate standby, empty Chianti bottles holding candles. (Decant the wine and serve it for dinner.) The green salad might also be present, as there is always some child who will eat nothing else.

Have simmering on the stove the two pots of sauces, each containing a ladle so that guests may serve themselves. At dessert time, present the surprise "pizza" in a pizza box and prepare the Zabaglione at the stove or, if the dining area is other than the kitchen, at the table over a portable burner.

Dim the lights and place a recording of Luciano Pavarotti singing Neapolitan songs on the phonograph. Distracting vocal music during mealtime is usually to be avoided, but in this party's general cacophony, it seems to fit nicely.

THE
MENU
(FOR 10)

Crostini

Fresh Pasta
Spiced Tomato Sauce with
Vegetables

Savory Green Sauce

Assorted Garnishes

Salad of Mixed Greens

Homemade Breadsticks

"Pizza"

Zabaglione

Wine: Chianti

CROSTINI

½ pound chicken livers
1 large onion, chopped fine
2 cloves garlic, 1 minced
1 stick unsalted butter, softened
1 tablespoon white wine
1 tablespoon minced parsley
2 tablespoons black Niçoise olives, minced
¼ cup Parmesan cheese, freshly grated
½ cup mayonnaise
Salt, pepper, nutmeg
15 slices firm white bread, crusts removed

PREPARE THE CHICKEN LIVERS by cutting off any membranes, then rocking a large knife repeatedly through the mass until it is well chopped.

Over low heat, cook the onion and minced garlic in 2 tablespoons of butter until they are soft but unbrowned. Press the onion against the side of the frying pan to drain off the fat, then remove onion to a bowl. In the remaining butter, sauté the livers briefly, allowing them to remain pale pink at the core. Again, press the livers against the side of the pan to strain off the plentiful juices, then combine livers with onion. Add the wine to the pan juices, turn up the heat, and reduce the liquid to 1 tablespoon. Add this glaze to the livers.

Purée the livers in a blender or food processor. Stir in parsley, olives, cheese, and mayonnaise. Add a scraping of nutmeg and some pepper, then taste for salt. Cover and refrigerate until needed.

To assemble, toast the bread on one side under a broiler. Lightly rub all toasted sides with a peeled clove of garlic. Butter the untoasted sides, then cut the slices across diagonally. Spread the liver mixture on the buttered side and place the Crostini under the broiler until bubbling and lightly browned. Serve at once. Serves 10

Pasta

5 large eggs, plus 3 egg yolks
2 tablespoons olive oil
1 teaspoon salt
4½ to 5 cups quick-blending flour (Wondra or Pillsbury's Sauce
  and Gravy Flour)

Note: if you do not possess or cannot borrow a pasta machine,
  then purchase a quality, Italian-made pasta such as DeCecco

INTO A LARGE MIXING BOWL, put the eggs, oil, and salt. Beat lightly
with a fork until the eggs are well blended. Start pouring in flour,
stirring all the while with a fork, until the eggs absorb sufficient flour so
that they appear to be a crumbly mass of dough. Press the dough
together with your fingers and turn it out onto a floured kneading
surface. Continue adding flour, kneading all the while until the dough
feels moderately firm and is no longer in danger of sticking to hands or
kneading surface. It is always easier to correct a slightly damp dough, so
don't allow it to become too stiff. Divide the dough into 4 portions;
wrap each tightly in plastic wrap; then cover the portions with a kitchen
towel and leave them, at room temperature, until needed. (Try to
prepare the dough no longer than 1 hour beforehand.)

Set the kneading blade of the pasta machine at its largest opening.
Roll a lump of pasta through and feel its consistency. If it seems at all
damp, press more quick-blending flour onto its surfaces. Fold the dough
into thirds, turn it so the folded sides are vertical, and run it through the
kneading blades again. (If the dough crumbles, it is over-dry; if it tears
along the edges, too much volume is being forced through the kneading
blades. In either case, cut down on the amount of dough that is being
worked.) Continue working the dough just until it has a slight sheen and
feels smooth to the touch. When novice pasta makers first try this, they
tend to over-knead, which toughens the pasta. Four to 6 kneads should
be sufficient if the consistency of the dough is correct. Keep an eye on
the process, for less kneading results in a finer product.

As soon as the dough feels smooth, start tightening the kneading
notches and work the dough progressively down until it reaches the last
or next-to-the-last notch. (Superfine pasta is difficult to cut on some
machines.) Stretch the sheets of pasta over laundry racks or broom

handles and allow them to dry, not to the point of crumbling, but rather to a slight toughening just along the outer edges.

Adjust the pasta machine to the desired cutting width and cut the pasta. Immediately sprinkle it with fine flour and toss the strands lightly about to loosen them. Cover pasta with a clean towel and continue until all is cut.

For a large party, fill 2 stockpots two-thirds full with well-salted water. Sprinkle a few drops of oil on the surface. Bring to a boil, then add the pasta in 2 batches, making sure it enters the water in more or less separate strands rather than in a bunch. Give a quick stir, cover the pots, and cook briefly (2 to 3 minutes at the most for *al dente* consistency). Strain out a piece and test taste it.

Drain well, then rapidly sprinkle the pasta with a few drops of olive oil before serving. Serves 10 with some extra

PASTA GARNISHES

Offer any or all of the following:

Chick peas, cooked according to package directions and lightly
    salted
Crisp, crumbled bacon
Large wedges of Pecorino and Parmesan cheeses, graters nearby
Anchovy filets, drained and blotted dry
Mushrooms, sautéed in olive oil that has been flavored with a
    crushed clove of garlic
Diced ham
Red peppers, broiled until their skins blister, then peeled and cut
    into thin strips
A bowl of loosely whipped cream
Bowls of chopped parsley and cut chives (or thinly sliced
    scallions)
Leaves of fresh basil in season, *or* preserved pesto sauce

Spiced Tomato Sauce with Vegetables

2 large onions, chopped
3 cloves garlic, minced
2 carrots, diced
2 stalks celery, diced
½ cup olive oil
4 pounds tomatoes in season, peeled, seeded, chopped, *or* 3 28-
    ounce cans Italian tomatoes
1 teaspoon sugar
⅓ cup red wine
⅓ cup chopped parsley
2 tablespoons mixed herbs (thyme, oregano, savory)
1 bay leaf
1 3-inch length of orange peel
2 teaspoons salt
¼ teaspoon cayenne, or to taste
½ teaspoon saffron
Freshly ground pepper
3 medium zucchini, sliced in rounds
1 small eggplant, cubed

IN A LARGE SAUCEPAN, slowly cook the onions, garlic, carrots, and celery in 3 tablespoons of oil until the vegetables are tender but unbrowned. Add tomatoes, sugar, wine, herbs, peel, salt, cayenne, and saffron. Simmer, uncovered, for 40 minutes, stirring occasionally. Remove the bay leaf and orange peel and purée the sauce in a food processor, or pass it through a food mill or press it through a sieve. Add pepper and taste for seasoning.

In the remaining oil, sauté first the zucchini rounds and then the eggplant. Press and strain the eggplant against the side of the pan and discard its excessive juices. Add the vegetables to the sauce. Make the sauce the day before and heat in a large pan when needed. Stir occasionally during the meal to make sure nothing is sticking.   Serves 10

SAVORY GREEN SAUCE

10 ounces fresh spinach
1 stick unsalted butter
8 tablespoons flour
4 cups milk
2 cups chicken stock, defatted
1 small onion, minced
1 bay leaf
Salt, pepper, nutmeg
2 cups grated Gruyère cheese
⅓ cup minced parsley
3 egg yolks
1 cup heavy cream, plus additional cream as needed

WASH AND STEM THE SPINACH. Place spinach in a large pot and cook, stirring constantly, in just the water clinging to the leaves. When the spinach is tender and still bright green, drain and refresh the spinach under cold running water. Squeeze the mass as dry as possible and chop well.

Melt 6 tablespoons of butter in a large saucepan, then whisk in the flour. Cook this roux over very low heat for 2 minutes, whisking constantly. Stir in the milk and stock. Add onion, bay leaf, salt, a light peppering, and a scraping of nutmeg. Let the sauce cook over the very lowest heat for 30 minutes. Occasionally pull the skin that forms over the surface to the side of the pan and discard it. Strain through a sieve. Stir the cheese, parsley, and spinach into the sauce. (The sauce can be done ahead to this point and refrigerated.)

Reheat the sauce if necessary. Mix egg yolks and cream and whisk in a ladle or 2 of the hot sauce. Add eggs to the saucepan and stir until well heated but do not allow to boil. Add cream as necessary to thin the sauce to a medium, coating consistency. Whisk in remaining 2 tablespoons of butter. Taste for seasoning and hold in a *bain-marie* or double boiler for service. Serves 10

Green Salad and Breadsticks

CHOOSE A VARIETY OF ROUGH GREENS for the salad: Romaine; escarole; arugula, if possible; and Boston or Bibb lettuce. Dress the salad with oil and vinegar touched lightly with garlic.

Make 1 recipe of Fresh Bread (page 142). After it has risen, punch the dough down and roll portions into fat breadsticks. Let rise for 15 minutes, then bake in a 350-degree oven for around 20 minutes.

Yields around 15 sticks

"Pizza"

Pie dough (pâte brisée; rough puff pastry (page 288); plain pastry)
Strawberry preserves
2 ounces white chocolate (Lindt or Suchard)
2 tablespoons ground blanched almonds
Trompe l'oeil candy black olives (optional)

"Pepperoni": ½ cup dates, pitted
5 ounces semisweet chocolate, grated
Pinch of ground cinnamon
1 cup pine nuts
¼ cup granulated sugar
1 tablespoon butter, melted
2 to 3 tablespoons honey
2 tablespoons cocoa
2 tablespoons confectioners sugar

PURÉE THE DATES in a food processor or chop them very well by hand. In a saucepan, combine dates, chocolate, cinnamon, nuts, and sugar and mix well. Drizzle on the butter and honey. Place the pan over very gentle heat and, using a hand, mix the ingredients until they soften

and adhere into a compact mass. Divide the mixture in half and roll each into a sausage shape. Mix cocoa and confectioners sugar on a plate and roll the 2 portions in the mixture until each is spottily coated. Wrap each sausage in aluminum foil and freeze for at least 1 hour or until completely hard. (As only 1 sausage is used per pizza, the remaining one can be kept frozen for another occasion.)

Preheat the oven to 350 degrees.

Roll out the pie dough to fit a large (15-inch) pizza pan and neatly flute the edge. Prick the dough over with a fork, then place a sheet of aluminum foil over the pastry and spread on a layer of dried beans to keep the crust as flat as possible while baking. Bake in oven for around 15 minutes, then remove the foil and beans and leave the pastry to brown and crisp for another 5 to 8 minutes. Remove from oven and cool completely.

To assemble the pizza, spread a thin layer of strawberry preserves over the pastry. Melt the white chocolate in 3 tablespoons of water then thin the chocolate, if necessary, with a few more drops so that it can pour thickly but smoothly. Slice the "pepperoni" and place around the pizza. Dribble on the melted white chocolate "cheese," then sprinkle the ground almonds about the surface as if some of the cheese had not melted. Add a few fake candy "black olives." Chill slightly.

Serve directly from the pizza pan by cutting portions with a pizza cutter. For more verisimilitude, beg a box from a pizza establishment and surprise guests by carrying it to table at dessert time stuffed with this *trompe l'oeil* confection.   Serves 10

Zabaglione

As the wedge of "Pizza" that is meant to accompany the following Zabaglione is relatively sweet, this recipe presents a slightly more tart version of the well-known Italian dessert than is usual.

4 whole eggs, at room temperature
4 egg yolks, at room temperature
⅓ cup granulated sugar
¼ cup sweet Marsala wine, or to taste

MAKE THE ZABAGLIONE in the classic rounded Zabaglione pot, or use a spotlessly cleaned copper egg-beating bowl or even a stainless-steel bowl. (The important thing is to have a rounded shape over which a whisk can move cleanly and smoothly.)

Place eggs, yolks, sugar, and wine in a bowl and begin whisking, with the bowl directly over low heat. (A hand whisk will take slightly longer and provide a bit more volume; an electric beater will get the job done faster but its noise may overwhelm the occasion.) Continue beating for 8 to 10 minutes or until the eggs are light and fluffy and certainly at least quadrupled in volume. Raise the bowl from the heat source as necessary to keep the eggs from cooking at the bottom of the dish. They need only be warm, not hot, as they expand. If you are whisking by hand, hold the bowl at its edge with a pot holder and beat first with the right hand, then turn the bowl and continue with the left.

Serve the Zabaglione as soon as it is finished. If the occasion is familial, hand out spoons and share from the bowl.   Serves 10

Celebrating Rituals of Winter

A
CHILDREN'S
COOKIE
PARTY

The Inspiration

. . . a set of chocolates in the shape of dominoes that I once purchased in a New York candy store.

First we played with the candy, setting up the small bars like a real game and smearing ourselves with chocolate in the process. Then we ate the game, thereby ensuring that both winners and losers—chocolate lovers all—won at least a gustatory victory. What, I wondered, would happen if one could create an entire meal that could be played with first, then eaten afterwards. The following children's Entertainment was devised with play in mind, and it has proved useful and delightful on many occasions.

Playing with food has long been a childish delight, and though parents tend to tire of the endless mess that young children make, it is this very play which serves as a child's introduction to sensory pleasure. The senses of smell, color, taste, and touch are all stimulated when a baby

A Children's
Cookie
Party

grasps and smears his banana, squishing it through his fingers and lovingly rubbing it in his hair. And it is the sensory and playful elements of food that most tempt a fussy youngster to eat. Children delight in spaghetti worms and meaty bones or asparagus because they can eat them with fingers, and things that go crunch in the mouth sound enchanting in their ears. They will, perversely, eat raw peas but not cooked ones, simply because they can shoot them about the tabletop like small, firm marbles. They will eat twice as many pancakes if you make them in the shape of Mickey Mouse instead of common rounds. In this Entertainment then, children are encouraged to play with their food as much as they like, and it is interesting to note that they will eat more at this party than they usually do at such events.

It is necessary that the children invited be at least five years old. I also find it helpful to limit the number of children at any juvenile gathering to a maximum of ten, although as in an adult dinner party, six to eight is to be preferred. The earlier in the day that a child's party can be held, the more likely that the occasion will be a successful one. Experience has also taught me that a two and one-half-hour party packed with activities is better than a three and one-half-hour party, the length of which toward the end of time tends to drive young and overexcitable egos to the collapsing point, thereby putting a certain pressure on a mother's tolerant good will.

As an adult party has its shape and form—its rising action, climax, and slowly dissolving culmination—so too does a child's party, but on such an occasion the action rises much faster, stays at a fervent pitch, then rapidly and totally disintegrates unless certain steps are taken to maintain decorum.

Setting the Scene

Have a time schedule for events and stick to it. Let children spend lots of time playing Tic-Tac-Toe and Pin the Tail, and lots of time eating sandwiches and relishes so they are not so hungry for deserts. (Incidentally, after they have eaten their sandwiches, it is amusing to point out to them that they have just eaten lots of crust and to watch the consternation on their little faces.)

After one hour of eating and decorating cookies and being good, there should be some free time in which the children can gallop about and be wicked. Let this time end in a free-for-all "snowball" fight. The last half-hour can be devoted to a coloring contest which will force everyone to settle down for a time and be still, and in such a state will mothers find their children when they come to pick them up.

As children tend not to notice their decorative surroundings so, with the exception of a few balloons, it has always seemed to me unnecessary to deck the halls with cut-outs and crepe paper. Hold the party, if you can, in a kitchen so that spills can easily be wiped from a vinyl floor. (Note also that the fruit punch is white in color rather than a staining red or purple.)

MENU AND SCHEDULE
(FOR 10 CHILDREN)

Tic-Tac-Toe Sandwiches

Pin the Tail on the Spaghetti Squash

Fruit Punch or Milk

Chocolate Dominoes

[Wipe off and Clean-up Time]

Gingerbread Jigsaw Puzzle

Checkers

Decorated Cookies

[Wipe off and Clean-up Time]

A "Snowball" Fight

A Coloring Contest

Tic-Tac-Toe Sandwiches

1 recipe Fresh Bread dough (page 142)
1 egg yolk
1 tablespoon water

Large piece of poster board
Red plastic tape

MAKE THE BREAD DOUGH and let it rise.

Punch the dough down and roll it out directly on a lightly oiled baking sheet to a thickness of 1-inch. To make bread Os, place a 6- or 7-inch saucer on the dough and cut around it with a sharp knife. Cut out a center plug of dough with a 3- or 4-inch cookie cutter. Make 5 Os, (more if there are more than 10 children). Let rise 20 minutes.

To make Xs, cut 1-inch-wide strips of dough, cross them, and smooth down the centers. They should be as tall and wide as the Os. Make 5 Xs, or more.

Preheat the oven to 350 degrees. Beat the egg yolk with the water and brush over the breads for a glaze. Bake the breads in oven for 20 to 25 minutes or until golden. It is a good idea to spray these breads with water from a plant mister 2 or 3 times during baking so they remain soft.

Cut a large square of poster board and divide it into 9 sections with red plastic tape. Let the children play the game, then slice the breads in two with a serrated knife, and let the children make sandwiches. For the sandwiches, offer:

Peanut butter
Grape jelly
Strawberry jam
Sliced cheese
Sliced bananas and brown sugar
Shredded lettuce
Chopped black olives
Mayonnaise
Butter

Help them make peanut butter, chopped olive, and mayonnaise sandwiches; or peanut butter and banana sandwiches sprinkled with brown sugar; or peanut butter and jelly sandwiches; or sliced cheese, lettuce, and peanut butter sandwiches; or any other bizarre combination they insist upon.

Pin the Tail on the Spaghetti Squash

1 large spaghetti squash
4 lemons
1 grapefruit
2 small yellow crookneck squashes
Pitted black olives
Parsley, washed and dried
Carrots, scraped and trimmed
Celery sticks

Bamboo skewers
Toothpicks
Lightweight green florist's wire
A kerchief for blindfold

THE SPAGHETTI SQUASH WILL FORM THE BODY OF THE ANIMAL. Trim off the pointed ends of the lemons. Cut 4 small, rounded indentations into the spaghetti squash and fit the lemons into them to act as legs. Attach lemons to squash by pushing long bamboo skewers up through the lemons and into the body. Attach the grapefruit at the stem end of the squash with skewers to form a head. Toothpicks can be used to affix crookneck squash ears, and 2 pieces of black olives can be attached to form eyes. Make a garland of parsley to hang around the animal's neck by gathering the stems and twisting florist's wire around the greenery. Drape around the joint of the neck and twist the wire ends together.

Place the beast on a large tray or cutting board. Slice carrots lengthwise (a mandoline is the best slicing tool), and fringe the broad ends of a few slices with a sharp knife. Drop carrots in ice water to crisp.

Arrange carrots, celery sticks, and pitted black olives (which little children like to stick on their fingers), in a bowl. Place toothpicks through the ends of the fringed carrots. Blindfold each child in turn and let him or her have a chance to pin a carrot tail on the spaghetti squash.

Fruit Punch

1 can (16-ounce) frozen lemonade
Juice of 2 lemons
Ginger ale
Ice cubes
20 maraschino cherries

DILUTE THE LEMONADE and lemon juice with 1 can of water, 2 cans of ginger ale, and 1 large tray of ice cubes. Float the cherries on top. Serve in paper cups.

Chocolate Dominoes

1½ cups granulated sugar
1⅓ cups cocoa
¾ cup all-purpose flour
Pinch of salt
Pinch of cinnamon
2 large eggs, lightly beaten
⅓ cup milk, plus 2 tablespoons
1 stick unsalted butter, melted

Chocolate glaze:
1 cup semisweet chocolate chips
½ cup butterscotch morsels
2 tablespoons water
¼ teaspoon vanilla extract
Confectioners sugar

PREHEAT OVEN TO 350 DEGREES. Grease a 9 × 13-inch baking pan and set aside.

Combine sugar, cocoa, flour, salt, and cinnamon. Make a well in the middle and stir in eggs and milk. When very smooth, add the melted butter. Pour into the greased baking pan and bake for about 40 minutes, or until the brownies are solid and dry at the center when tested with a toothpick. Let cool, then cut into 20 rectangles. Place the rectangles on a rack for easy frosting.

Over hot water, melt the chocolate chips and butterscotch morsels. Let cool slightly, then spread all but 2 tablespoons of the chocolate over the top of the cookie bars. Place the remaining chocolate glaze into a twisted paper cone (see Note), and draw lines through the center width of each domino. Let cool and harden at room temperature.

Mix water, vanilla, and enough confectioners sugar to make a small amount of medium-thick frosting. Place the white frosting in another paper cone or an icing bag and dot on the numbers of the dominoes. To serve, arrange the dominoes like a played game on a doily.

Paper Piping cone

To make a paper piping cone, cut wax or parchment paper into a triangle 12 × 12 × 16½ inches. Lay the triangle on a counter, with the long end toward you. Bring the left point up, twist it under, and curve the point to meet the top of the triangle. Bring the right-hand point up and over and twist it around to the back to meet the top of the triangle. All 3 points will now fit together and a sharply pointed cone end will be opposite them. Fold the points down and together in 3 or 4 pleats so they will remain stable, then fill the bag no more than half full. Cut off the pointed tip of the cone with scissors, gather the top portions of the bag together, and press gently to form design.

The following Gingerbread recipe will make 1 large jigsaw puzzle *or* 1 checkerboard and extra dough for cookie shapes to frost. If the cookies will be kept and stored rather than eaten, toughen the dough by substituting the cheapest margarine available for the butter and use only 3 teaspoons of cinnamon for the spice.

GINGERBREAD DOUGH

2 sticks unsalted butter
1⅓ cups dark brown sugar
¾ cup sugar
3 large eggs, lightly beaten
½ teaspoon salt
1 teaspoon cinnamon
2 teaspoons ground ginger
½ teaspoon allspice
6 to 6½ cups all-purpose flour
1½ teaspoons baking soda
½ cup hot water

Cardboard or heavy paper

CREAM THE BUTTER and the sugars together in a large bowl, then stir in the beaten eggs. Sift together the salt, spices, and 6 cups of flour. Dissolve the baking soda in the hot water. Stir baking soda mixture and flour mixture alternately into the butter until well blended. The dough should be quite firm. Cover and refrigerate overnight.

If the dough seems at all soft before it is to be formed, knead in more flour to strengthen it.

HARD WHITE FROSTING

2 egg whites
1 teaspoon lemon juice
½ teaspoon vanilla extract
Confectioners sugar

Food coloring
Artist's brushes
Pastry brushes

BEAT THE EGG WHITES until just slightly frothy. Add lemon juice and vanilla. Place a sieve over the bowl and pour in confectioners sugar. Sieve and stir in sugar until the frosting reaches a smooth glaze of medium consistency.

GINGERBREAD JIGSAW PUZZLE

SELECT THE LARGEST BAKING SHEET that will fit in your oven. The puzzle pattern should be 1½ inches less in width and length than the baking sheet to allow for the expansion of the dough in baking.

Assume we are working with a 17 × 14-inch baking sheet. Cut a sheet of cardboard or heavy paper to a rectangle measuring 15½ × 12½ inches. Make a jigsaw puzzle pattern of 12 interlocking sections by

drawing out the puzzle on the paper. (A pattern from a child's puzzle can be copied and enlarged.) Make the interlocking rounds and angles large and broad. Cut the paper puzzle into sections.

Preheat the oven to 325 degrees.

Lightly grease the back of a baking sheet (so no rims will be in the way of rolling), and roll out the dough directly on the sheet to an ideal thickness of ¼ inch. The dough will tend to be overthick in the middle unless special care is taken to smooth it evenly to the edges. If the dough splits at any point, lightly moisten a small portion of dough with a bit of water and press it over the split.

Assemble the cardboard puzzle on top of the dough. With a small, sharp knife carefully trace around each puzzle piece and around the edge of the puzzle as a whole. Place the cookie in the oven and bake for 15 minutes, then remove the cookie and, with a sharp knife, trace and cut carefully around all the puzzle lines. Let bake for another 35 to 40 minutes. Remove from the oven and immediately cut around the puzzle sections again. Gently separate and remove the sections to cooling racks.

When the portions are completely cool, brush all loose crumbs from the pieces and frost with Hard White Frosting.

Reassemble the cookie puzzle on a clean baking sheet. Using a pastry brush, coat the puzzle with frosting until it is as smooth and white as possible. Leave to harden in a dry place for a good 3 hours or overnight.

Cut out a paper rectangle as large as the cookie puzzle, and draw a design on it that you find pleasing. (The easiest design is a 1½-inch border and a single, rustic figure or animal that can be cut out and traced directly on the cookie with a brush dipped in food coloring.) Use this paper pattern to practice before painting on actual puzzle.

Mix food colorings on a plate to desired shades and dilute with water until they are pretty and pastel. Paint the puzzle with artist's brushes for details, and with pastry brushes where wide swatches of color are needed. To make a dark outlining shade, mix green and slightly more red to a pleasing brown.

If the puzzle is to be preserved, dip each section in clear polyurethane and let dry for a hard, finishing varnish.

GINGERBREAD CHECKERBOARD

1 batch Gingerbread (page 245)
½ recipe Hard White Frosting
Red food coloring
6 ounces semisweet chocolate
Rounds of red licorice (1 inch in diameter)
Chocolate rounds (1 inch in diameter; Droste's Pastilles are
    perfect)

Artist's brush

PREHEAT THE OVEN TO 325 DEGREES. The checkerboard should be 14 to 15 inches square. Select your largest baking sheet and, greasing the back side, roll out the dough directly on the greased sheet. Roll to an even ¼-inch thickness. Using a ruler, mark off the 14- or 15-inch square, then cut the dough, allowing a minimum ½-inch border around the edge. Bake in oven for around 35 to 40 minutes. Let cool briefly, then slide the square onto a cake rack and cool completely.

Make a half batch of Hard White Frosting, and tint it pink with food coloring. Divide the gingerbread into 8 rows and 64 squares. If the cookie is 14 inches square, each square will be 1¾ inches. Using a ruler and an artist's brush dipped in frosting, place a dot at each point of measurement. Brush the pink frosting with a wide pastry brush on every other square (never mind exact lines and corners). Let the pink frosting dry completely, then brush over the frosting with a light coating of diluted red food coloring. Let dry.

Melt the chocolate over hot water. Brush the chocolate neatly over the unfrosted squares and use it to define the red squares. When dry, place the checkerboard on 4 paper doilies. (A large heavy piece of cardboard can be used for support if so desired.) Use red licorice and chocolate rounds for playing pieces.

COOKIES FOR DECORATING

CUT ALL REMAINING DOUGH into a variety of shapes and bake as cookies for the children to decorate. Provide an assortment of dragées, sprinkles, and garnishes and 2 colors of Browned Butter Frosting.

BROWNED BUTTER FROSTING

1 stick unsalted butter
4 tablespoons heavy cream
2 teaspoons vanilla extract
4 cups sifted confectioners sugar, approximately

MELT THE BUTTER in a saucepan over low heat, and let it turn a pale nut brown. Immediately stir in the cream and vanilla, then add confectioners sugar. The frosting should be of peanut butter consistency. Divide the frosting into 2 portions and tint one pale yellow and the other pale pink. Cover tightly with plastic wrap until needed.

A SNOWBALL FIGHT

GIVE EACH CHILD 2 large puffs of cotton batting and let them throw them at each other, preferably out of doors.

A COLORING CONTEST

HAVE LONG LENGTHS of brown wrapping paper. Let each child lie down on the paper, then quickly trace his or her body form with a wide-tipped felt pen. Rapidly add hair, facial features, and a few clothing outlines. Provide crayons and let the children color themselves, then cut out the figures. Give small prizes to each child for the best figures: the most original, colorful, funniest, scariest, neatest, weirdest, and so on.

When each child goes home, he or she carries a self-portrait and a bag containing a prize, licorice, chocolate checkers, and a piece of the jigsaw puzzle.

An Early American Tea

The Inspiration

. . . the enticing description of a bountiful Dutch country tea in Washington Irving's "Legend of Sleepy Hollow."

It is easy, perhaps, to forget that the gentle ceremony of tea-taking was once as prevalent in America as ever it was in Europe, and that it was the Dutch, not the English, who first imported tea in 1610 and who introduced tea to the continent. From Holland, the custom of afternoon tea crossed the Atlantic to New Amsterdam (later to be rechristened New York). It was there, precisely in New Amsterdam and in the stately parlor of the Van Tassel family mansion, that Washington Irving stopped the story of Ichabod Crane, the unfortunate suitor of the Van Tassel's daughter, long enough to describe the ample charms of a genuine Dutch country tea table:

> Such heaped-up platters of cakes of various and almost indescribable kinds, known only to experienced Dutch housewives: There was the doughty doughnut, the tenderer *oly koek* (a cake fried in deep fat), and

An Early
American
Tea

the crisp and crumbling cruller;
sweet cakes and short cakes, ginger
cakes and honey cakes, and the
whole family of cakes. And then
there were apple pies and peach pies
and pumpkin pies; besides slices of
ham and smoked beef; and
moreover delectable dishes of
preserved plums, and peaches, and
pears, and quinces; not to mention
broiled shad and roasted chickens;
all mingled higgledy-piggledy . . .

Now this tea was meant to provide a
full meal for a great many people, and it
little suggests the insipid fare that one
usually equates with a modern tea. As the
motherly teapot spouted clouds of vapor
and old Baltus Van Tassel moved good
humoredly among his guests, gossip and
music and dancing filled the long, sweet
hours of the evening. The Mistress Van
Tassel, a most socially correct grande
dame, served many varieties of tea brewed
in different pots, both to please her guests'
tastes and, at the same time, to show off
the wealth of her silver closet. She did not
mix the tea with milk or cream (that was a
French fashion that would arrive in years
to come), but she did offer, in a "bite-and-
stir" box, lumps of expensive sugar and
pistils of saffron and peach leaves which
guests could steep in their tea for
flavoring.

Ichabod Crane, Irving records, did
ample justice to every dainty on the table.
And though he later lost the heiress
Katrina Van Tassel to Brom Bones and

was chased from Sleepy Hollow through the dark night by a Headless Horseman, never to be seen again, I've always thought that Irving at least meant us to know that Ichabod rode off to his fate on a full stomach and was, perhaps, comforted by the feast before his fall.

Setting the Scene

A full, formal tea can be one of the most elegant Entertainments possible, for it provides the opportunity to draw from dark cupboards those delicate heirloom dishes that so many families possess but rarely put to use. A romantic tea setting is easily obtained by using old lace of crocheted clothes, (one of the better buys at antique stores), over plain cotton or woven underclothes. Make informal bouquets of old-fashioned flowers, particularly anemones, snapdragons, and roses, and pin up the edges of the lace into scallops by attaching roses in hidden Water Pics. Crowd the table with a wealth of dishes heaped with food and fill any remaining spaces to overflowing with objects like paperweights and candlesticks. If possible use two tables, one for tea and one for food. Load the tea table with cups, saucers, teapots, and an extra pot containing hot chocolate for any children present. Make a "bite-and-stir" box from a partitioned dish or place several small baskets on a serving tray. Fill the partitions with various sugar lumps and place some peach or hibiscus leaves in the center for flavoring if they are in season. An old-fashioned tea is a good generation-spanning meal, for both young and old enjoy these mildly sweet foods. If, however, hungry men are attending at mealtime, an added roasted bird or two would not go unappreciated.

A tea should be served in the best parlor, or perhaps even placed in the front hall to surprise and delight guests. It is a perfect occasion at which to play or listen to chamber music.

THE
MENU
(FOR 12 TO 15)

*Oly Koek (Oil Cakes) with
Cinnamon Sugar*

Ginger Cakes

Apple Butter Tarts

Peach Tarts

Raisin and Honey Scones

Assorted Jams and Jellies

*Cucumber and Watercress
Sandwiches*

Grated Radish Sandwiches

Roasted Chickens (optional)

Hot Chocolate

Tea

Lemon Wedges

A Bite-and-Stir box

GINGER CAKES

2 sticks unsalted butter
1 cup dark brown sugar
3 large eggs, slightly beaten
½ cup honey
½ cup corn syrup
2 teaspoons ground ginger
1 teaspoon allspice
4 or 5 scrapings of nutmeg
3 cups all-purpose flour
1 teaspoon baking soda
1 tablespoon hot water
Confectioners sugar
Candied red cherries

PREHEAT THE OVEN TO 350 DEGREES.

Cream the butter and sugar, and stir in the eggs. Add honey and corn syrup and mix well. Sift together the spices and flour and stir into the egg mixture until a smooth batter evolves.

Dissolve the baking soda in hot water and add to the batter. Pour into a buttered 9 × 13-inch baking pan. Bake in oven for around 45 minutes or until firm in the center. Let the cake cool, then cut into 15 squares. Dust lightly with sieved confectioners sugar, and lift the squares out of the pan. Place a red cherry half on top of each portion.

Makes 15 cakes

OLY KOEK (OIL CAKES) WITH CINNAMON SUGAR

1½ envelopes dry yeast
2 tablespoons sugar
3 tablespoons water
1⅓ cups milk, slightly warmed
3 cups unbleached flour
1 teaspoon salt
2 large eggs, beaten
2 tablespoons chopped dates
1 tablespoon chopped, candied citrus peel
2 teaspoons grated lemon zest
Peanut oil for frying
Cinnamon sugar

DISSOLVE THE YEAST and sugar in water, then stir in the warm milk. Place flour and salt in a large mixing bowl. Make a well in the center. Alternately add the milk and eggs, and continue stirring until a very smooth batter forms. Mix in the dates, peel, and lemon zest. Cover the bowl with a towel and set in a warm place for 1½ hours to rise.

Heat oil to 370 degrees. (Test by dropping in a piece of batter; it should sizzle and bob rapidly back up to the surface.)

Do not stir down the batter. Lift out tablespoon-sized portions of batter onto an oiled spoon and drop them into the oil. Do not overcrowd the pan. Fry for around 5 to 6 minutes or until the cakes are nicely browed on all sides. Lift out with a slotted spoon and drain on paper toweling.

When all the cakes are fried, they can be set aside, then reheated slightly in a warming oven before serving.

Place a bowl of cinnamon sugar near the cakes so that guests can dip their fritters in the mixture.   Makes around 30 cakes

APPLE BUTTER TARTS

2 pounds tart, flavorful apples (Winesaps,
  Cortlands, Jonathans, etc.)
1 cup apple juice
2 cups light brown sugar
1 teaspoon cinnamon
¼ teaspoon allspice
Pinch of cloves
2 tablespoons lemon juice

Pie crust: 1½ sticks chilled, unsalted butter, cut in morsels
2 cups all-purpose flour
Large pinch of salt
1 teaspoon sugar
¼ cup ice water, approximately
Stiffly whipped cream

TO MAKE THE APPLE BUTTER, wash, core, and slice the apples (do not peel). Place apples and apple juice in a stainless-steel pan and simmer until the apples are purée soft. Press the apples through a sieve or food mill.

Return the purée to a heavy pan and add sugar, spices, and lemon juice. Cook over very low heat and stir frequently until the pulp thickens to the point of barely moving. Let cool. This recipe makes around 5 cups of apple butter. Whatever is not used for the tarts can be offered at the tea along with other assorted jams and jellies, and the remainder can be refrigerated and kept for future use.

To make the pie crust, rapidly combine the butter, flour, and salt with your fingertips to an even, small-flaked mixture. Drizzle ice water over the flour and gather the dough into a ball. Give 1 or 2 quick kneads to smooth the dough, then wrap it in foil or plastic wrap and refrigerate for 30 minutes.

Preheat the oven to 350 degrees.

Roll out the dough and either fill tartlet molds or make rimmed, free-form tart cases on a baking sheet. (I like a generous 4-inch tart.) Prick the bottoms of the tarts with a fork and bake in oven for around 20 minutes or until golden and crisp. (Check the tart cases half way through baking and deflate and press down any portions of dough that threaten to rise unevenly.) Cool the pastries.

Spread and smooth a thick layer of apple butter into the tart cases. Just before serving, pipe a small rosette of whipped cream in the center of each tart.   Makes around 15 tarts

Peach Tarts

4 tablespoons unsalted butter
4 tablespoons vegetable shortening
1 cup granulated sugar
1 egg
1¾ cups all-purpose flour, sifted after measure
2 teaspoons baking powder
3 tablespoons ground almonds
1 cup peach or apricot preserves
Confectioners sugar

PREHEAT THE OVEN TO 350 DEGREES.

Cream butter, shortening, and sugar until light and smooth. Stir in the egg. Combine flour, baking powder, and nuts and stir into the butter mixture. Mix until just blended; overworking the dough will toughen it.

Roll out the dough to a thickness of ⅛ inch on the back of a lightly greased baking sheet. Cut 3-inch circles. In half the circles, cut out a small tulip shape with a cookie cutter or freehand. Gather the scrapes of dough and continue to roll and cut until all the pastry is used.

Bake in oven for around 12 to 15 minutes, or until the shapes are just slightly golden at the edges. Remove and let cool.

Place the preserves in a small, heavy pan and let them simmer and thicken over low heat for 10 minutes. Push through a strainer and let cool.

To compose the tarts, sieve a thick layer of confectioners sugar over the pastries with the cut out designs. Spread preserves over the solid rounds and then place the sugar-strewn halves on top.

Makes 12 to 15 cookie tarts

RAISIN AND HONEY SCONES

4 cups all-purpose flour, plus additional flour as needed
¼ teaspoon salt
1 tablespoon baking powder
1 stick unsalted butter, chilled
⅓ cup golden raisins
⅓ cup muscat raisins
½ cup honey
½ cup milk
⅓ cup heavy cream
1 egg yolk
1 tablespoon water
Granulated sugar

PREHEAT THE OVEN TO 450 DEGREES.

Sieve together the flour, salt, and baking powder. Cut the butter into morsels and work it rapidly into the dry ingredients with your fingertips, until a flaky mixture of oatmeal consistency results. Mix in the raisins.

Combine honey, milk, and cream, and heat until just slightly warm. Make a well in the middle of the dry ingredients and pour in the milk. Rapidly combine liquid and dry ingredients to a malleable dough. Turn out the dough onto a floured counter and briefly work it, adding a bit more flour as necessary until the dough feels stiff enough to roll. (The dough should have a heavy, gingerbread quality about it.)

Flour the rolling pin and roll out the dough directly onto a lightly greased baking sheet. Form a 12-inch circle that is a good 1-inch thick. Pat into shape with your fingers. Cut the dough into 12 to 14 wedges, scoring the marks deeply through the dough but not disturbing its circular form.

Beat egg yolk with water and brush the glaze over the top of the scones. Sprinkle with sugar and bake in oven for around 25 minutes. Immediately run a knife over the indentions to separate the scones.

These are good served just slightly warm. Have a mound of unsalted butter next to the scones so that guests can butter their breads.

Serves 12 to 14

CUCUMBER AND WATERCRESS SANDWICHES

>2 small cucumbers, peeled
>Salt
>1 bunch watercress
>2 scallions, white parts only, chopped
>1 stick unsalted butter, softened
>Ground pepper
>12 to 15 slices firm white bread

Garnish: 1 small cucumber, washed

CUT THE 2 PEELED CUCUMBERS in half lengthwise and scoop out the seeds. Grate the cucumbers through a Mouli julienne grater or in a food processor. Salt lightly and leave to drain for 30 minutes. Squeeze the gratings by handfuls until they are very dry.

Pick the green leaves and tender stems from the watercress. Purée watercress, scallions, and butter in a blender or food processor until it is

a smooth, green mash. Stir in the cucumbers. Add pepper and taste for salt. Chill the mixture.

Cut the bread into crustless rounds or squares. Spread on the cucumber mixture. (If desired, these sandwiches can be topped with another slice of bread.)

Cut thin garnishing slices of unpeeled cucumber. Cut each slice two-thirds of the way through, twist the slice into a pretty curve, and place it on top of the sandwich.   Makes 12 to 15 sandwiches

GRATED RADISH SANDWICHES

2 large bunches radishes, washed and trimmed
Salt
1 stick unsalted butter, softened
½ cup mayonnaise
Ground pepper
12 to 15 slices firm white bread
Small parsley sprigs

SELECT 5 OR 6 PRETTY RADISHES and cut them into thin slices. Set aside. Grate the remaining radishes through the number 3 blade of a Mouli julienne hand grater or a food processor. Lightly salt the radishes and let them sit for 30 minutes. Drain radishes and, taking the gratings up by handfuls, squeeze them 2 or 3 times until they are as dry as you can get them. There should be around 1 cup of gratings.

Mix together radishes, butter, mayonnaise, and pepper. Taste for salt and add more if needed, then put the mixture to chill.

Cut the bread into large, crustless rounds. Arrange the slices on a baking sheet and lightly toast one side under a broiler. When cool, spread the radish mixture on top. Place a small sprig of parsley and 3 radish slices in the center of each sandwich.

These should be served chilled. They can be composed up to 3 hours before needed, covered with plastic wrap, and kept in the refrigerator.
                    Makes 12 to 15 good-sized sandwiches

A MAPLE SUGAR-HOUSE BREAKFAST

The Inspiration

. . . the New England sugarhouses that open wide their doors to visitors at syrup boiling time.

It is not until late-breaking winter, when the ground begins to thaw, that the sap runs sweet again. And it is as if the pleasant soul of nature, held hidden deep within the earth throughout the nadir of the year, springs vital up the roots of the maples. Then men bore and tap the trees, drive in spigots and hang them with buckets, and the sap gives freely of itself, like a sweet pledge of mild months to come. The sugarers collect the sap and, in a ritual as old as America itself, they carry it to sugarhouses and there, over hot fires, boil it down, evaporating quantities of thin maple sap to produce single gallons of pure amber syrup.

In Massachusetts and Vermont, you can drive into the countryside and small signs will direct you to the sugaring

A Maple
Sugarhouse
Breakfast

houses. Often they are open to visitors throughout the day and frequently, all day long, they serve breakfast. Come in from the cold and sit at long tables and watch the evaporators; and the steam from them and the fires lit in old oil-drum stoves and stone fireplaces will warm you to the quick. While men tend the syrup, their womenfolk cook for you, always pancakes and waffles, bacon and eggs, but also homemade doughnut balls, and maple cakes, and sticky fritters lowered into hot syrup after they are fried. Ask for Sugar on Snow, and chances are that a woman will order one of the children away from his checker game to go out in the sugar bush and collect the snow. When the child returns, with the snow heaped in a bowl, he will throw off his boots and jacket and resume his game, and the odor of wet wool will blend with that of frying bacon and the permeating sweetness of the syrup.

Throughout the morning, people collect in the sugarhouse. There are an old man or two in checkered shirt and suspenders, puffing on a pipe and saying little; growing boys consuming plate after plate of breakfast; small children looking glassy-eyed from too much sweetness, from having been allowed to pull great masses of syrup off the snow where it hardened to a sticky taffy. And there are adults who, in the warmth and comforting abundance, sense with nostalgia the specialness of place and slow, gentle time.

Setting the Scene

This repast, which could be served at breakfast time or for an elongated brunch throughout a morning, ideally will be set before a fireplace. Spread a red and white checkered cloth over a table and place on it those elements that can be served buffet style. Have card tables for people to eat at, or one long table, again covered with a checkered cloth where people can sit.

If this meal is to be served as a brunch, it is necessary that someone act as short-order cook. (If a great many guests are slated to come, consider hiring a professional to whip up eggs and bacon and pancakes to relieve you of the task.)

Buy some inexpensive dime-store washcloths. Soak them in scented water, wring them dry, then fold them once and roll up. Place in a pan in a warming oven and hand them around when everyone is finished with Sugar on Snow.

Offer a great many board games scattered around the room for people to play during and after the breakfast.

Have a pot of water with 2 tablespoons of cinnamon simmering on the stove before guests arrive to scent the air with an old-fashioned fragrance.

THE
MENU
(FOR 10 OR MORE)

Fried Eggs

Bacon or Sausage

*Stuffed French Toast with
Pure Maple Syrup and
Whipped Unsalted Butter*

Ebelskiver Pancakes

*Sugar on Snow with Dill
Pickle Wedges and Unleavened
Wheat Crackers*

Buttermilk Doughnut Holes

*Ruth's Grated Apple Cake
with Maple Streusel*

Coffee, Hot Chocolate

Games

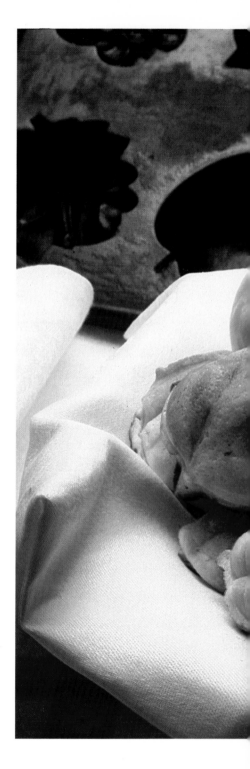

STUFFED FRENCH TOAST

Thick slices of firm white or egg bread, ¾ inch thick
Raspberry or strawberry preserves
Eggs
Milk
Salt
Vanilla extract
Cornflakes cereal, slightly crushed
Unsalted butter and vegetable shortening for frying
Whipped butter
Pure maple syrup

TRIM THE CRUSTS from the bread slices and cut slices in half diagonally. With a small paring knife, make a slit in the middle of the long slanted side of the slices and move the knife until a pocket forms. Leave the 2 shorter sides of the slices intact. Spoon some jam into the slits.

Crack eggs (use 1 large egg for every 4 half-slices of bread) into a dish and add 3 tablespoons milk per egg. Season with a pinch of salt and a drop or 2 of vanilla per egg. Lightly beat with a fork until well blended, and dip in the slices of bread. Let them absorb a goodly amount of egg.

Place the cornflakes on a plate and press the bread slices lightly into the cereal, which need not be dense upon the bread.

Heat a mixture of butter and vegetable shortening in a large frying pan and fry bread until crisp and golden brown. Serve at once with whipped butter and maple syrup.

EBELSKIVER PANCAKES

24 Domino Dot sugar cubes
Cinnamon
2 cups cake flour
½ teaspoon salt
1 teaspoon baking powder
4 large eggs, separated and at room temperature
1 tablespoon sugar
2 cups minus 2 tablespoons milk
4 tablespoons unsalted butter, melted

THESE PANCAKES CAN BE COOKED in a classic wrought-iron ebelskiver pan with its rounded indentations, or in any other iron pan ranging from a cornstick mold to an antique muffin mold as shown in the picture on page 271. The batter can also be spooned onto a hot griddle in small portions if no suitable mold can be found.

Lightly grease the mold and wipe it clean with paper toweling. The mold should be placed directly over a medium heat to warm just before the pancakes are begun.

Moisten each sugar cube with a drop or 2 of water and roll them in cinnamon.

Sift together the flour, salt, and baking powder.

Beat the egg yolks and sugar until light and thick. Add the dry ingredients, alternating with the milk and butter and stir until a smooth batter forms. Beat the egg whites until they form stiff glossy peaks, then fold them into the batter.

Fill the molds half full with batter and let them cook over medium-low heat until the pancakes pull away from the side of the mold and appear set and browned on their undersides (around 10 minutes for large pancakes).

Press a sugar cube into the soft interior of each pancake, then pry the pancakes from the mold with a fork. Add a small spoon of batter to each mold and immediately place in a pancake, unbrowned side down. Cook another 5 minutes or until brown. Regrease the pan lightly between batches.   Makes about 24 pancakes

SUGAR ON SNOW

Snow, or a large bag of ice
2 to 3 cups pure maple syrup

PACK THE SNOW on a large round platter and mound it up into the semblance of a mountain. (If using ice, finely crush it bit by bit in a food processor before pressing into shape.) Hold in a freezer until needed.

Place the syrup in a saucepan with sides tall enough so there is no danger of the syrup's boiling over. Clip a thermometer to the side of the pan and heat the syrup to 270 degrees. Have a large bowl of ice water by the side of the stove and immediately, when the syrup hits the degree mark, place the bottom of the pan in the water to stop the rising temperature. (If you have no thermometer, gage the temperature in the following way: Have a cup of cold water by the pan. As the syrup heats, it will also thicken; watch for this visual sign. Place a drop of syrup in the cup. Look for the stage at which it forms a soft ball (245 degrees) which can be manipulated with the fingers. At 250 degrees, a hard ball will form which will feel firm to the touch. At this point, the temperature will rise rapidly. At 270 degrees, the soft crack stage occurs and the dropped ball of syrup should form a thin skin which will crack slightly. Remove the pan immediately and cool its bottom.)

Rush snow and syrup to table and pour out the syrup over the snow, swirling it round and round. Each diner reaches into the mass of syrup with a fork and pulls and stretches out his or her toffeelike bite.

With Sugar on Snow, serve dill pickle wedges to help cut the syrup's saccharine intensity, and crackers to help dislodge the sticky candy from the teeth.

Unleavened Wheat Crackers

⅔ cup whole wheat flour
1 cup all-purpose flour, plus additional as
    needed
1 teaspoon salt
1 teaspoon sugar
4 tablespoons chilled, unsalted butter, cut in
    morsels
Cold water

Glaze: 1 egg yolk
2 tablespoons cream
Kosher or flaked sea salt

PLACE FLOURS, SALT, AND SUGAR in a bowl and blend well. Add the butter and, using your fingertips, work it into the flour until it disappears and the flour has a uniform, slightly grainy texture. Stirring the flour all the time with a hand, add sprinklings of cold water until the mass can be compacted neatly into a firm dough. Knead gently and briefly. If you are rolling crackers out by hand, make a slightly softer dough. If you have a pasta machine, the dough must be firm enough to pass through the blades without sticking, and more flour can be added in the rolling process if necessary. Cover the dough and set aside for 30 minutes.

To roll out by hand, divide the dough into 3 portions. Roll each out on a floured surface, sprinkling the dough and rolling pin with more flour as necessary, until a large round circle is formed no thicker than ¼ inch at any point. Transfer to an oiled baking sheet and prick lightly with a fork. Cut a hole in the center. Make 3 oversized crackers from which guests can break portions.

To roll through a pasta machine, set the kneading blade at its widest opening. Divide the dough into 2 portions and pass each through the blade. (Press the dough into plain flour as necessary if it feels at all sticky.) Continue feeding the dough through the machine, tightening the blades 1 step each time, until you reach the third notch from the end.

The dough can now be cut into small circles, or you can overlap the 2 strips on an oiled baking sheet, compact the joint with the rolling pin, and cut large circles. Prick with a fork.

Beat the egg yolk with the cream to form a glaze. Brush over the crackers and sprinkle with salt. The crackers should sit for 15 minutes before baking. Preheat the oven to 350 degrees.

Bake crackers in oven for 15 minutes or until lightly golden around the edges. Transfer to a cooling rack, and when the crackers are at room temperature, store in a tightly covered box. These are best served within a day.

BUTTERMILK DOUGHNUT HOLES

2 cups all-purpose flour
½ teaspoon baking powder
½ teaspoon baking soda
½ teaspoon salt
A pinch of cinnamon
6 scrapings of nutmeg
1 egg
½ cup sugar
2 tablespoons unsalted butter, melted
½ cup buttermilk, at room temperature
1 quart oil for frying (peanut or other vegetable oil)
Pure maple syrup

SIFT TOGETHER THE FLOUR, baking powder, soda, salt, and spices. In a bowl, beat the egg and sugar until well blended. Add the melted butter and buttermilk. Stir in the dry ingredients and mix to a very smooth dough. Cover and refrigerate for 30 minutes.

With lightly oiled hands, take up portions of the dough and roll them into small balls no larger than 1 inch in diameter. Let the balls rest on a floured counter for 10 minutes while the oil heats.

Heat oil to 375 degrees in a deep fryer or a pan with tall sides. Place in an uncrowded layer of doughnuts and let them fry for around 3 minutes, turn the balls as necessary so they brown on all sides. Lift out with tongs and place on absorbent paper to drain. Immediately add more balls to maintain the temperature of the oil correctly.

These doughnuts are best served fresh and hot or at least reheated. Heap them up on a pedestaled cake stand and pour a drizzle of maple syrup over the holes.   Makes around 3 dozen doughnut balls

Ruth's Grated Apple Cake with Maple Streusel

¾ cup unsalted butter
1 cup sugar
½ cup pure maple syrup
4 eggs, lightly beaten
3 cups all-purpose flour
½ teaspoon salt
1 teaspoon baking soda
3 teaspoons baking powder
2 tablespoons buttermilk
3 to 4 apples (firm, tart eating apples like
   Winesaps)
Confectioners sugar

Streusel:
¼ cup butter
½ cup brown sugar
⅓ cup all-purpose flour
1 teaspoon cinnamon
¼ cup pecans or walnuts, ground
¼ cup pure maple syrup

PREHEAT OVEN TO 350 DEGREES. Butter a 10-inch springform cake pan and set aside.

Cream the butter and sugar together. Stir in the maple syrup and then the eggs. Sift flour, salt, soda, and baking powder together and add to the egg mixture. Stir in the buttermilk.

Core the apples (do not peel) and grate through the medium hole of a hand grater or the #3 blade of a Mouli julienne grater. There should be 1½ cups of apple. Stir apples immediately into the cake batter. Pour batter into the prepared cake pan.

To make the streusel, combine butter, brown sugar, flour, cinnamon, and nuts. Work with your fingers until a crumbly mixture forms, then drizzle maple syrup over the mass and mix to a medium crumb. Scatter the topping evenly over the cake batter. Bake the cake for 1 hour, then test the center with a toothpick. If the center seems at all moist, leave the cake for another 10 minutes. Remove from the oven and cool.

Trace a 10-inch circle on a sheet of paper. Cut out the circle and fold it in half 3 times. Make a rough doily by cutting a design along the folds and scalloping the long edge. Unfold and place the doily on top of the cake. Sieve confectioners sugar over the top, then carefully lift off the paper to reveal the design.   Serves 10 to 12

A PROVENÇAL CHRISTMAS

The Inspiration

. . . the traditional Provençal end-of-year celebrations.

Starting at Christmas, they stretch through the New Year and on to January 6 and Epiphany, that occasion when first, presumably, the Christ Child was presented to the Magi and his divinity made manifest.

If Le Grand Aïoli springs from and celebrates the fruitful abundance of high summer, then the Provençal Christmas *réveillon* likewise honors the staples of winter—those dependable, often common foods that sustain a people throughout the dark season of the year. Dried fruits, glacéed fruits, nuts, root vegetables, seafood, and garlic, always garlic, combine into a menu of traditional dishes eaten after the family attends midnight Mass; garlic soup, perhaps snails or other seafood with aïoli, provincial pastries like sweetened spinach tart or *Pompe à l'Huile*, a thick, flat almost cookie, prepared with an olive-oil dough.

At New Year's, the celebratory foods are apt to be more formal, less common.

A
Provençal
Christmas

It is truffle season in France, and fresh *foie gras* is available. What could better accompany the occasion when one must see a new year in with Champagne.

The Epiphany celebration is a particularly joyous one, for it entails the eating of the Twelfth Night Cake or the Cake of the Kings (*Gâteau des Rois*). The cake itself is usually a brioche or savarin creation, and hidden deep within it is a dried *fève* (broad) bean or a silver coin. At the end of the meal, the cake is cut into: one symbolic sliver for the Infant Jesus, another for his mother, portions for the Magi, and the rest for the guests. Whoever receives the bean or coin is cheered and crowned with a gilt diadem. That lucky person becomes the host for the next evening. At his or her house, then, is the feast repeated and the new king or queen crowned; and throughout the month of January, in a self-perpetuating feast, the *fêtes* continue, dictated always by the bean. (The simple coin or ring hidden in a humble food is found in many cultures at holidays: the mounded Irish potato dish Colcannon holds a ring and coin on All Saints' night; the English Christmas Pudding might embrace a penny along with its plums and currants; and Hoppin' John always hides a New Year's coin in the South.) It is a simple celebration, but one that binds family and friends together, and it holds one additional pleasure. When your turn as host is finished, you can relax and let your friends provide the entertainment from then on.

Setting the Scene

This party combines both Christmas and Epiphany celebrations. The menu is a light soup, followed by a great many quiches and bready tarts, all Provençal in leaning, and thirteen Desserts of Christmas. Note that it provides an easy feast for many people and that it would do nicely for a holiday open house. The soup could be kept warm on the stove (guests would serve themselves a cup), and two buffet areas—one for quiches, one for desserts—could be arranged elsewhere.

Use strings of Christmas lights and shiny glass bulbs around the desserts. Tuck into the fruit display some wax candle fruits and light them. Use, if you wish, small-print Provençal materials for tablecloths.

Purchase an inexpensive golden crown from a costume shop and have it ready for the king or queen. For an added, very French touch (particularly at a family gathering), have a toasting session with the Champagne. Write on slips of paper the names of all other guests. Let everyone, children included, draw one name before the feast and then prepare a short toast, a small gift of pretty, kindly words, to be presented later.

MENU
(FOR 16 TO 20)

Cream of Garlic Soup
Spinach Tart
Ham and Asparagus Quiche
Tomato and Herb Pizza
Parmesan Pizza
Pumpkin Bread

The Thirteen Desserts of
Christmas

Gâteau des Rois
Raisins
Prunes
Dates
Glacéed Apricots
Grapes
Tangerines
Apples
Pears
Pistachios
Pine nuts
Walnuts in the Shell
Silver Candied Almonds or
Jordan Almonds

Wine: Châteauneuf-du-Pape or
Tavel Rosé with the main
course
Champagne with Desserts

Toasts

CREAM OF GARLIC SOUP

40 large cloves garlic, peeled and roughly
    chopped
2 large onions, chopped
5 tablespoons olive oil
6 tablespoons all-purpose flour
2½ quarts hot milk
4 large all-purpose potatoes, peeled and diced
2 sage leaves
1 bay leaf
Salt and pepper
6 egg yolks
1⅓ cups whipping cream

Croûtons: a baguette or thinly sliced white bread
Olive oil
Salt
1 garlic clove, peeled

COOK GARLIC AND ONIONS in olive oil in a large, covered pan. Let the garlic gently sweat until it is soft, and make sure that it does not brown.

Sprinkle the flour over the garlic and onions and continue stirring for 3 minutes until the vegetables appear to be a thick, smooth paste. Whisk in the hot milk, add sage, bay leaf, and seasoning, then bring to the boil. Immediately reduce the heat to a mere simmer and cook, covered, for 15 minutes. Stir occasionally.

Strain the soup base through a sieve. Pick out the herb leaves, then push through all the vegetable matter. (The soup can be prepared ahead to this point.)

Beat the egg yolks and cream together. (Reheat soup base if necessary.) Slowly add 3 or 4 ladles of hot soup to the eggs, then pour the eggs into the soup. Cook over gentle heat, stirring constantly until it thickens just slightly. Do not allow to boil. Adjust the consistency with additional milk if necessary to form a soup of light cream consistency. Adjust seasoning. Give everyone a small mug or bowl of this soup, and float a crouton on the top. Additional croutons can be offered in a basket.

Serves 16

To make the croutons, slice the bread Melba-toast thin or cut 2-inch rounds of thinly sliced white bread (there should be at least 2 per person). Generously coat a baking sheet with olive oil. Place the slices on the tray and brush the tops with more oil. Sprinkle with salt. Bake in a very slow (200 to 250 degrees) oven for a good hour or until the toasts are crisp, dry, and slightly golden. Give each crouton a quick swipe with the peeled garlic clove. These can be stored the day before in a tight container, then reheated slightly before serving.

OLIVE OIL PASTRY

The following pastry can be made up in a large batch and it will serve to line both the spinach and ham tarts. The addition of olive oil to the pastry makes it particularly Provençal in flavor.

6 cups all-purpose flour, approximately
1½ teaspoons salt
2 sticks unsalted butter, chilled and cut in morsels
1 cup good quality olive oil
Cold water
1 egg white beaten to a froth with 2 tablespoons water

PLACE THE FLOUR AND SALT in a large bowl and mix together. Add the butter and work it into the flour with your fingertips until it disappears. Sprinkle the oil over the flour and continually mix with your hands until a ragged dough appears. Sprinkle on tablespoons of cold water as needed and work the mass into a cohesive ball of dough. Give the dough 2 or 3 kneads, wrap it in foil, and chill for at least 30 minutes.

Preheat the oven to 350 degrees.

Roll out the dough on a floured surface to a thickness of ⅛ inch. Fill 1 large traditional quiche dish, and a 14-inch sided pizza pan. (Save remaining scraps to make lattice covering.) Prick the pastry with a fork and place a layer of foil over and into the pastry. Half fill the tarts with dried beans.

Bake tart shells in the oven for 15 minutes. Remove from the oven and lift out the beans and foil. Brush with beaten egg white. Place the shells back in the oven for 5 minutes to dry, then remove and add fillings.

Makes 2 large tarts

SPINACH TART

3 pounds fresh spinach, washed and stemmed
Salt and pepper
4 tablespoons olive oil
3 large cloves garlic, finely minced or pressed
1 tablespoon sugar
1 teaspoon finely rubbed dried oregano
1 teaspoon dried thyme
6 eggs plus 2 egg yolks
3 cups heavy cream
Nutmeg
6 ounces good feta cheese, crumbled
1 egg yolk beaten with 1 tablespoon water

PLACE THE SPINACH IN A LARGE POT, salt it lightly, and cook over brisk heat in only the water clinging to the leaves. Constantly stir the spinach, lifting the wilted leaves up and pushing the uncooked leaves down until the whole mass is tender. Turn out into a colander, refresh with cold water, and press out all moisture. Run a stainless-steel knife through the spinach until it is finely chopped.

Heat oil in a large skillet. Add garlic, swirl the pan briefly, then add sugar, spinach, and herbs. Stir rapidly over brisk heat until the spinach absorbs all the oil. Remove from heat.

Preheat the oven to 350 degrees.

Whisk together eggs, cream, a few scrapings of nutmeg, 1 teaspoon of salt, and generous pepper. Crumble in the feta cheese. Spread the spinach evenly over the surface of the pastry in the pizza pan. Pour over the eggs and cream. Roll out and cut 6 long, inch-wide strips of pastry and place them in a diagonal lattice pattern over the filling. Press the edges of the pastry strips and rim together.

Brush beaten egg yolk mixture over the pastry. Put tart to bake in the oven for 45 to 50 minutes or until nicely browned.   Serves 12 to 15

Ham and Asparagus Quiche

2 cups sliced asparagus, plus 7 whole stalks
2 tablespoons olive oil
1 medium-small onion, chopped
2 cups diced ham
6 eggs plus 2 egg yolks
3 cups whipping cream
Salt and pepper
Nutmeg
⅓ cup grated Gruyère cheese
½ teaspoon grated horseradish (optional)
5 to 6 small, canned tomatoes

PREHEAT THE OVEN TO 350 DEGREES.

Bring a pot of salted water to the boil. Bend and break the whole asparagus stalks at their tender point. Parboil the stalks until just tender and still bright green. Lift out the stalks on a strainer and rinse them immediately with cold water. Set aside. Add the sliced asparagus to the water and parboil until tender but still crunchy. Drain and refresh under cool water.

Heat oil in a frying pan and sauté the onion for 5 minutes. Add the diced ham, sauté for another minute, and remove from heat.

Mix eggs, cream, 1 teaspoon salt, pepper, and a few scrapings of nutmeg in a large bowl. Stir in the cheese and optional horseradish. Add sliced asparagus and ham. Pour mixture into the traditional pastry-lined quiche dish. Put to bake in oven for around 25 minutes or until the egg is beginning to set at the edges but is still slightly soft in the middle.

Cut out any tough stem ends from the tomatoes and press them gently, rounding them into neat shapes in the process. Remove the quiche from the oven and carefully arrange the tomatoes and asparagus spears into a pleasing pattern on the top. Return the quiche to the oven and continue baking for another 20 to 25 minutes, or until completely firm and golden.   Serves 10 to 12

You can, if you wish, make the following pizzas on risen and thinly rolled Fresh Bread dough (page 142), but the very best Provençal pizza is made in bakeries on a thinly rolled puffed pastry. Shoveled into massive, brick-hearth ovens when the bread is finished, these pizzas always have a delicious, slightly charred quality about them.

ROUGH PUFF PASTRY FOR PIZZAS

3½ cups flour, preferably unbleached
1 teaspoon salt
3 sticks unsalted butter, chilled and cut in ½ tablespoon pieces
Ice water

MIX FLOUR AND SALT IN A BOWL. Add the butter and rapidly work it into the flour with your fingertips. Stop working in the butter when it has uniformly been broken into still visible, almond-sized slicks. Sprinkle a ½ cup of ice water over the pastry, mix it in rapidly, then continue to add spoonfuls of water until the dough can be pulled together in a neat ball. Give 1 or 2 quick kneads (the butter needs to look unincorporated at this point), wrap the mass in foil, and refrigerate for 20 minutes.

On a floured surface, roll out the dough to a rectangle approximately 9 × 12 inches. Square up the corners as much as possible, and sprinkle any sticking slicks of butter with a bit of flour. Fold the dough over into thirds. Turn the dough on the table so its length is perpendicular to you and roll again into a large rectangle. Fold into thirds. You have now given the pastry 2 turns. Wrap in foil and refrigerate for at least 30 minutes.

Roll the pastry out again and give it 2 more turns as in the previous paragraph. Rewrap and let rest for 30 minutes to overnight.

You can, if you wish, give 2 more turns to the pastry, but a total of 4 is quite sufficient for rustic pizza. Roll out the dough as thinly as possible (aim for a good ⅛ inch). Transfer to a pizza pan or large baking tin, and cut a 14- or 15-inch round. Let the dough sit for 15 minutes before spreading it with sauce.   Makes 3 large pizzas

Tomato and Herb Pizza

½ recipe Spiced Tomato Sauce *without* added zucchini
    and eggplant (page 227)
½ teaspoon fresh or dried thyme
½ teaspoon fresh or dried oregano
1 large round of Rough Puff Pastry
French or Greek oil-cured black olives

AFTER THE SPICED TOMATO SAUCE HAS BEEN PURÉED, place it back in a heavy saucepan, add thyme and oregano, and reduce it over medium heat by half so that it is like a tomato paste in consistency. Stir the sauce frequently to avoid scorching it. Taste carefully for seasoning.

Preheat oven to 375 degrees.

Spread the sauce over the entire pastry round. Bake for 40 to 45 minutes.

Parmesan Pizza

1½ cups freshly grated Parmesan cheese
1 large egg
Pepper, nutmeg
1 clove garlic, peeled and pressed
Heavy cream
1 large round of Rough Puff Pastry
Olive oil

PREHEAT THE OVEN TO 375 DEGREES.

Mix cheese, egg, pepper, 2 or 3 scrapings of nutmeg, garlic, and enough cream to produce a substance that is spreadable and almost peanut-butter thick. Spread the cheese mixture over the pastry, leaving 1 inch around the rim free. Drizzle 2 or 3 tablespoons of oil over the surface, and put to bake in oven for 40 minutes or until speckled and pleasingly golden.

To serve, cut each pizza into 8 or 10 portions. Arrange the pizzas alternately on platters so that there are 2 pretty red and yellow arrangements. Place a black olive at the center edge of each red portion.

Serves 16 to 20

Pumpkin Bread

1 batch Fresh Bread dough (page 142)
1 cup pumpkin purée
2 eggs
½ cup grated Gruyère cheese
⅓ cup heavy cream
½ teaspoon freshly grated black pepper
½ teaspoon salt
2 or 3 scrapings of nutmeg
2 small whole bay leaves
Olive oil
1 egg yolk beaten with 1 tablespoon water

MAKE THE BREAD DOUGH and let it rise once. Punch the dough down and place it on a large oiled baking or pizza pan. Roll the dough out with a rolling pin until it reaches roughly a 14-inch circle. Let the dough rise again for 30 minutes.

Mix pumpkin purée, eggs, ¼ cup cheese, cream, and seasonings until blended. Preheat an oven to 375 degrees.

When the dough has risen, take a floured glass tumbler and roll over the dough from the center out to the edge, but do not roll over the edges. Rather, compress the interior and slightly spread the dough outward until a small plump rim forms at the edge of the bread. Immediately fill the indentation with the pumpkin mixture and sprinkle with the remaining cheese. Arrange 2 bay leaves in the center and drizzle a bit of olive oil over the surface. There should be 1 to 1½ inches of plain bread around the exterior. Brush this edge with egg yolk and water glaze.

Place bread in the oven for 45 to 50 minutes or until the pumpkin center is firm and the exposed crust is nicely browned. Serve slightly warm and cut into wedges.   Serves at least 12

GÂTEAU DES ROIS

½ cup raisins
2 tablespoons light rum
1½ envelopes dry yeast
3 tablespoons sugar
¼ cup warm water
⅔ cup milk, warmed
3⅔ cups sifted flour, preferably unbleached
¾ teaspoon salt
7 large eggs, lightly beaten, at room temperature
1 teaspoon finely grated lemon zest
2 sticks unsalted butter, melted and cooled

1 clean, shiny dime
A 12-cup savarin or ring mold
Buttercream Frosting

PLACE RAISINS, RUM, AND ¼ CUP WATER IN A SMALL PAN. Bring to a simmer and let cook over gentle heat until the raisins are plump and the liquid has evaporated. Set aside.

Dissolve yeast and sugar in water. Stir in the milk.

In a large bowl, mix the flour and salt. Make a well in the middle and add yeast, eggs, and lemon. Mix the liquid elements with your fingers, then slowly incorporate more and more of the flour until a moist dough forms. Pour in the melted butter gradually, and keep working the dough with your hand, pulling it away from the side of the bowl, stretching it out, kneading it hard, until after 6 to 7 minutes it gains a certain elasticity. Cover the bowl with a slightly damp towel and put to rest in a warm place for 1 hour.

Blot the raisins almost dry and moisten the dime with water. Sprinkle these solids lightly with flour. (Bakers call these solid objects within dough "heavy carriers." Coating them with flour allows them to maintain position throughout the dough rather than sinking to the bottom.)

Sprinkle the raisins over the dough, punch the dough down, and work it briefly until the raisins and dime are well incorporated within the mass.

Generously butter a savarin or ring mold and place in the dough. Make sure the dime is deep within the center and lost to sight. Cover the pan with a damp towel, and let rise in a warm but not hot place until the dough almost reaches the top of the mold.

Bake cake in a 375-degree oven for 40 minutes. Let the cake cool slightly, then turn it out from the pan. Sprinkle lightly with rum if you so desire, and pipe on a frosting design.

Small servings for 16 to 20 people

BUTTERCREAM FROSTING

1 large egg, at room temperature
2 tablespoons sugar
¼ teaspoon vanilla extract
1 stick unsalted butter, at room temperature

Pastry bag with rosette tube

WHISK EGG, SUGAR, AND VANILLA until they form a very thick sponge. Cream the butter in the bowl of a mixer. Beat the egg mixture into the butter in 2 or 3 portions. If the buttercream looks at all curdled, let the mixer continue beating and the frosting will soon right itself.

Place the frosting in a pastry bag with a small rosette tube. Pipe 2 circles of frosting around the top of the cake, then join the circles with a series of short cross strokes to that a pretty buttercream ladder encircles the rim.

APPENDIX: ON DECORATING DINING ROOMS

When we first considered buying our present home, the dining room was the least appealing room in the house. The living room had possibilities, the entryway and staircase character, and the kitchen begged to be used and lived in, but the dining room suggested nothing and inspired one not at all. A small room it was, in a house built in the days when all houses had to possess a formal dining area, be it ever so minute. And there it sat, just off the front entry, with one door leading in, another door leading out to the kitchen; two plain windows; and fifteen-foot-square dimensions. Impossible, I thought. What could one ever hope to do with 125 square feet and an eight-and-one-half-foot ceiling?

In time the living chamber composed itself and the kitchen turned into a dream, but the dining room simply remained there. It had its table, its surrounding chairs, a corner cupboard holding plants and plates, but it never came to life in any meaningful way. Time and again I chose to entertain and eat within the warm informality of the kitchen rather than subject guests to the claustrophobic sterility of that small, white room.

As I thought about my decorating dilemma, considered friends' dining rooms, and examined interior design magazines, I became increasingly struck by the notion that other people frequently did not know what to do with their dining rooms either. Continually one observed the formal table, the matching set of stiff-backed chairs, the carefully placed floral arrangement (frequently artificial) between two stalwart candlesticks. At the room's edge often stood a sentry sideboard hung with untouchable family heirlooms looking far too good to use, while overhead hung the grandest, prismatic chandelier affordable, its stark, remorseless light casting down upon the table, food, and guests.

How the norm contrasted with the vision I had of what a dining room *should* be! I thought of those golden, glowing restaurant rooms of France; those elegant, flowered *intime* chambers that bespoke romance, where one always feels more beautiful, more alluring. My drab room was even the antithesis of the cheery French bistro, less formal in spirit than its more elegant counterpart, but brighter, happier, always more seductively focused on the food. Where was there a more studied, successful approach to the psychology of conducive eating places than a restaurant? Why shouldn't one use all the tricks of those glamorous places one's self? That dramatic, golden aura was what I wanted, but how was it possible to accomplish such a feat in such a stunted space?

Functioning then as my own decorator, and moving slowly, step by step (certainly in no reasonable or organized manner), I began to wrest that small room from enclosed drabness into open light. The first priority was apparent: expand the space. As there was no way for the room to grow in size, mirrors were the only answer. One or two hanging mirrors were not going to do the trick, however; what was needed was a much bolder move: the mirroring of entire walls. (Fortunately there was chair railing and picture molding already around the room; had they not been there, I would have added them at this point.) To keep down expenses I purchased self-affixing mirrored-glass squares from a department store and simply started covering the upper walls. Moving cautiously, I began first by doing two adjoining walls. The room expanded and moved outward, but it soon came up against the blank flatness of the walls opposite, and there it stopped dead. With some trepidation I moved on, mirroring the third, then the fourth wall (a professional glass cutter trimmed the necessary small mirrors to fit at corners and around window frames). Now the whole room opened dramatically, catching and holding small portions of the red hallway, spilling over into the kitchen; the windows doubled and light glittered and bounced unchecked about the room. As the mirror material was inexpensive, the reflection it gave tended to be refracted brokenly, so to help quiet this effect and to give a more professional finish to the surface, I purchased from a hardware store those decorative brass "buttons" that are used with nails to hold heavy mirror in place. These were attached at each corner with short, hidden strips of double-faced adhesive tape.

Now not only did the room appear to quadruple in size, but also the mirrors added a certain psychological drama to the atmosphere. It is for many reasons that French restaurants add mirroring to their rooms. Consider the Parisian *fin de siècle* restaurants Lassarre or Maxim's, where there was little need to enlarge already spacious rooms; instead, the mirrors were used to aid romantic intrigue. (The Professional Beauty sitting at dinner with a lover glances across the room; there, seated at table with another partner but staring straight ahead into the mirror, with eyes watching only her, is a handsome man. Throughout the meal eyes catch and hold, unbeknownst to the partners unless . . . could they too be holding a small ocular affair? The opportunities were unlimited: to the right, to the left; glancing eyes, flirtatious eyes; eyes across the roses, veiled eyes lifting from a glass of wine; Beauty preening herself reflected . . . and now it could happen in my very dining room!)

Once the mirrors were in place, it became necessary to paint and color the walls and molding. But why mute the vision with a bland béchamel of white? First I painted the walls a glossy clotted cream, the rich tone I tried to remember from French restaurants. Livelier but still too bland, I painted again, this time with a cream so dark it bordered almost on yellow. The paint was mixed to order: a white base with yellow, gold, and light orange pigment added until I said stop. Over this, on the walls between baseboard and chair railing, I hand-rubbed a darker melon tone to produce a stippled effect. This time the aura was perfect. It is a decorator's truism that yellow walls enrich everything enclosed within their space, that yellow holds and can absorb an amazing number of colors against itself. The entire atmosphere now turned to candlelight yellow, one of the nicest shades that can reflect against the skin. (If the room is painted ever again, I would try apricot shell, a pale terra cotta, or an audacious pumpkin for their flattering tones.)

Now the ceiling was all wrong, for, lowering and plain, it seemed to dominate the room. It needed to be vaulted, sent skyward somehow. With a quart of the palest azure paint and perched on a ladder, I worked my way across the ceiling, leaving the outer edges of the room the darkest blue, then adding a bit of white to lift the heavy center and leaving, here and there, delicate spots of white as if the sheerest clouds had drifted across a sky made endless by the mirrors. (Yes, had I been clever enough to paint the heavens first, it would have saved me from having to scrape portions of it off the room's clean walls.)

Wishing to have at my fingertips the greatest range of lighting effects possible, I had installed two sconces on each windowless wall. As there was no wiring in the walls, a small hole was drilled at a meeting corner of four mirrors, a toggle bolt inserted, and the sconce screwed into the bolt. An unobtrusive cord then extended down the wall to an electrical outlet. The sconce lights, all naked bulbs, were covered with small shades the color to cast an ivory light. (The French often sew a shell-pink satin inside their shades to lend a warming glow, but whether or not this step is taken, it is most necessary to unabashedly throw a boudoir light upon the dining area. Use pink or cameo light bulbs— whatever is necessary to cast the spell—and all lights should also be on rheostats (dimmer switches) for instant, turn-of-the-hand control. The chandelier of *faux* bamboo entwined with green enameled leaves I also shaded, as nothing is more unflattering than a raw blue shadow casting down upon the face. Were it possible to rewire the room, I should have liked to have added a recessed theatrical spot directly above each table. With all other lights off and a dark cloth upon the table, it would have been possible to highlight a simple centerpiece with dazzling efficiency.

A weeping fig and a rubber tree were moved into the two opposing corners under the sky, and were in turn expanded by the mirrors into a small forest of twelve reflected trees. They also provided an interesting lighting phenomenon. When inexpensive up-turned spotlights were settled on the floor beneath the trees, the leaves and branches appeared in shadow tracery upon the ceiling-sky.

The shell of the room was now finished, and what was evolving—what I intended to evolve—was a small restaurant right in my own home . . . a room that would still be saved for company or more important family occasions, but one that called upon every trick of the professional restaurant for its decorative appeal. Now the long, prosaic table down the center of the room looked totally out of place. Fortunately, that table could be expanded with six extra leaves, but for the time being, I contracted it to a small oval and pushed it to one side. That left room for another table: a large round one in the opposite corner (again the mirrors quadrupled the tables in spirit, if not in reality). To make optimum use of space, two cushioned banquettes were constructed, free-standing objects of five-and-a-half- and six-foot lengths that provided seating directly against two walls, thus allowing a working aisle between the two tables. When the table before the banquettes was expanded, ten people could just fit around its length. If the table was contracted, it provided a cozy, cushioned corner for a tête-à-tête. Again, a bit of the psychology of the restaurant occurred; after the rich meal, after the warming wines, see the Professional Beauty almost at a recline on the soft, yielding bed of her banquette.

Other seating solutions had already been thrust upon me: a set of four black, cane-seated chairs; and a set of six Chinese Chippendale chairs that could be finished in any manner one chose. Now all that remained were the decorative touches of choosing curtains, fabric for the banquettes, and tablecloths. Here another dilemma arose. Obviously one needed a rich and elegant room for formal occasions, but would that same room really do for more casual situations when peasant fare was in order? If the room was rich and heavily swagged for elegant times, would that same look not be mightily out of place in the summer? And what about those meals when exotic foods were served . . . a North African couscous under prisms and amid the silver? What was needed was a totally adaptable room, using several easy decorative schemes to fit many different culinary motifs and seasons—four different stage sets if you will, each made as dramatic as space and money would allow. As it turned out, the monetary outlay for all of these sets was remarkably low. I purchased two bolts of material; three changes of tablecloths; about $100 worth of wood furring strips to make trellising; some simple window treatments; and, at varying times, different greenery. The remaining elements—rugs, dishes, paintings—I already possessed, and they were scattered here and there about the house.

The Exotic Dining Room

The Exotic Dining Room was the easiest to compose. It does not, perhaps, ring true to any culture, for it is a mix of East Indian, North African, and Oriental artifacts, but the overall effect has a tented and opulent flavor that is particularly persuasive in the evening. It is an appropriate setting for dim sum, curry, and couscous, and I would not hesitate to try a bit of seduction here either. The banquettes are covered with their permanent fabric, a rusty red with a small gold motif. There are several throw pillows of leopard-patterned needlepoint and various batiks. The banquettes are thrust apart at the corner so that a small bamboo table fitted between them can hold a potted palm and an antique basket. At various points about the room, and affixed to the picture molding by means of hooks and spring rods, are six hanging Indian-print bedspreads with gold backgrounds; two are looped together in the corner behind the small table holding the palm. If the ceiling were a bit higher, I would tack even more cloths to the molding and gather them in around the light fixture into a tented canopy.

The tablecloths are more Indian-print spreads. The round table in the corner is twice covered, with an underskirt of Indian-print cloth and, draped over it, an antique paisley shawl with knotted corners. On the floor is a zebra-skin rug fetched from the study. The Chinese Chippendale chairs are around the tables (I settled on a coat of bamboo-

tan lacquer and an upholstery fabric of patterned greenery and large red flowers.) Every brass candlestick in the house is used, and two brass trays—each set upon a lazy Susan—provide revolving centerpieces from which guests can help themselves to condiments. The dishes are a mixed set of blue and white English stoneware, with an array of inexpensive Chinese bowls and cups added. Starched white napkins loosely gathered in the center then pushed through brass napkin rings are placed at each setting.

The windows are topped with draped curtains made from the same material that covers the banquettes. Hooked just under them are tortoise-shell shades. To add a golden red aura, three thirty-nine-cent tie-dyed scarves are draped over the center light. The far corner, seen reflected in the long mirror, is filled with plants and illuminated by a floor spotlight. An hour before guests are due, a musk-scented incense stick is lit, placed in the center of the room.

The Trellised Gazebo

The most dramatic change in the dining room occurs in the summertime when light lingers there throughout the long day. Stripped from the windows are the bamboo shades, the heavy curtains, and all other draped vestiges of that rich red color; everywhere, the attempt is made to brighten and lift the eye. The fabric that sets the tone for the room is the same as is used on the Chippendale chairs. Its bordered pattern is the only one necessary to set the room's tonal qualities: it appears as underskirting on both tables; it is sewn on padded cushions which are tied in place on the backs of chairs; it is cut into lengths and held in place by the same picture-molding method that attached the swagged red curtains. The fabric also covers the banquette backs in the easiest of Velcro snap-together ways, and it slipcovers the banquette cushions. To lighten the floor, the straw matting from the kitchen is placed at the room's center, and its open, woven design nicely complements the fabric's border and the trelliswork.

From furring strips, a carpenter constructed five pieces of trellising, each five feet long and two-and-one-half feet wide. Rather than paint the trellis with the same flat tone as the molding, I rapidly spray-painted them by holding a can of white enamel in one hand and a can of yellow in the other, quickly swirling both paints over the surface of the raw wood, which produced a slightly mottled and interesting effect. These frames were tacked to the molding and chair railing using the very smallest of nails. It was now possible to stand in the room and count fifteen distinct portions of trellising reflected in the mirrors.

On the tables were starched white cloths and napkins, white dishes with green Portuguese pottery accents, and baskets of greenery and

flowers the same colors as those in the fabric. In order to suggest a greenhouse atmosphere, I placed as many plants as possible around the room. The banquettes remained sufficiently separated to allow the weeping fig in the corner. The opposite corner has a variegated-leaf rubber tree with two large ferns at its base. Another large plant sits at the end of the banquette by the kitchen door, but I still needed more plants. My carpenter then made for me two removable "window ledges" with neatly rounded edges. Long screws dropped through both ends and down into holes drilled in the actual window sills, and I could then place more small plants along both windows without cutting into the floor or seating space of the room itself. To further the verdant atmosphere, I purchased a sixteen-inch wreath frame from a florist and cut it with a knife at one point. Using one-inch-long wooden floral picks, I wrapped the pick's wire around two galax leaves and covered the entire frame with greenery. Twisting the wreath at its cut point, I could then easily fit it around the light fixture and suspend it from the chandelier chain with wire.

One hour before guests are due, I add extra-fresh ivy and wire on a few roses, each preserved within a water pic, to the light fixture. Then I briefly light a floral Porthault candle.

The Informal Bistro

The Bistro Dining Room draws upon and intensifies the qualities of blue within the room. As blue can be a rather unflattering color both to food and to guests, it is necessary that it be offset with enough red and yellow light to disperse its cool and artificial characteristics. The basic red fabric that upholsters the banquettes is used to swag one corner and the two windows, and, to supplement, ten red geranium plants in full bloom are placed along the extended window ledges, around the base of the corner rubber tree, and on the dessert serving table. Viewed in the mirrors, they completely encircle the room. On spring rods at each window are lace café curtains which nicely mellow the incoming light.

The floor remains its plain oaken self, and the chairs used are the set of black, cane-seated chairs gathered from around the house. From the living room comes the blue and white china collection, twelve plates and platters with their hangers attached, which are then hooked to the mirrors by means of stick-on picture holders.

Just as the china is a mix of pattern and shade, so the tablecloths continue the variety. Checked and patterned undercloths are topped with appliquéd cloths, and pillow slipcovers in a variety of blues enclose those same pillows seen in the exotic setting. As the banquettes are now pushed together at the corner, the largest blue pillow serves to

camouflage the section where otherwise a blank portion of the wall would show.

I particularly like to use a restaurant service formula in this setting. The antique menu holder, usually found in the kitchen, is placed at the room's entry to announce the evening's selection of dishes. A small, rolling, marble-top table is brought from the kitchen, topped with a white cloth, and used to hold a variety of desserts from which people can choose. (Or, one might start the meal with a cart of various hors d'oeuvre from which to select.) Guests are then encouraged to rise and help themselves.

Starched white napkins, folded in half and gently pleated, are fanned in wine glasses. Red candles and peasant pottery complete the bistro's informality. At night this setting is lit as brightly as possible. Ten minutes before guests are due to arrive, I boil up a small pot of water which contains 2 teaspoons of cinnamon, then place the pot at the room's center to perfume the air.

The Formal Dining Room

The final dining room arrangement is a spectacular nighttime presentation that depends mostly on lighting effects for its visual impact. I find this setting especially useful around the holiday season for small, one-table dinner parties or, when the room is striped of all chairs, for a display area at an elegant buffet meant to serve a very large group. (Drinks are available in the kitchen, plates and silver are set upon the round table, savory dishes served from the long oval table. After the main course, platters are quickly cleared and coffee is then offered from the round table while the oval table holds an assortment of desserts.)

Visually there is glitter, glitter everywhere—all frankly fake—and to set it off most effectively, the room's lower framework is darkened as much as possible. The floor is covered with a rust-colored carpeting the same tone as the banquettes. The tables are draped in lace and covered with the whitest clothes and napkins, so that the linens almost float in pristine contrast. The mirroring on two walls is darkened but at the same time glamourized by the addition of a series of gold-framed paintings of food, as if it were a small gallery. The artwork lends some of the charm found in civilized English clubs, where artful etchings hang by scores upon upholstered walls. Floor lights shine up to highlight some of the paintings.

In two corners stand plants covered with small, white Christmas lights. Outside the windows, propped up in two large flowerpots, are branches of fir trees, each covered with another strand of glowing lights. The white lampshades on the lighting fixture are exchanged for black, so

that their large orbs of light do not overpower the small lights. Hanging from the lamp and shades, and also from the sconces, are an abundance of prisms—some new, some antique—all catching and amplifying light.

This is the dining room in which to use roses as centerpieces and vast bouquets on the peripheries. Although I don't particularly like them elsewhere, gladiolas are a perfect formal "French restaurant" flower, and they provide the most quantity and color for the least money. With this setting, I like a sharp evergreen scent. A Cyprus candle by Rigaud is lit one hour before guests arrive. Only a trace of its evocative odor remains, but it quickly alerts guests to the festive, holiday spirit.

And what of the mundane dining room, the room that is there every non-entertaining day? It too is set in one of these four fashions. The dishes and glasses are always upon the table, the napkins wait in place, and every morning when I rise and pass through the room on the way to the kitchen, I am moved with anticipation. Only the silver needs to be laid . . . just a few delicious flowers centered on the tables. My spirit lightens, for in no time at all a party could be possible. What a promising way to start every day.

INDEX